Advance Praise for

Pause

"*Pause* is the real deal. With proven techniques backed by science, Rachael O'Meara shows us how to connect with ourselves and tap into what we really value."

—Arianna Huffington,
New York Times bestselling author of *Thrive*

"Pausing can add wonderful value to your life. In this enlightening book, Rachael shares many useful tips and inspiring stories that show how to tune in to your life, align yourself with your passions, and live with meaning. This is truly a book worth pausing for." —Chade-Meng Tan,
bestselling author of *Search Inside Yourself*
and *Joy on Demand*

"*Pause* is a much-needed and timely book for those of us who often feel stuck or whose to-do lists have taken over our lives. The lessons, stories, and insights Rachael shares will help you discover the practical and powerful value of pausing. In this step-by-step guide, she shows you how to return to the wisdom of your natural flow in your daily life."

—Agapi Stassinopoulos,
bestselling author of *Unbinding the Heart*
and *Wake Up to the Joy of You*

"Rachael O'Meara has captured a critical component of a life well lived—taking periodic pauses, or time-outs, to realign our actions with our inner voice. Career pauses—whether one minute, one day, or one week—are the essential ingredient to making meaningful next moves." —Jenny Blake,
author of *Pivot: The Only Move
That Matters is Your Next One*

"*Pause* is a wonderful guide to living our lives with more courage, self-compassion, and authenticity. Rachael shows us how to tap into our deeper selves and notice what is happening underneath the surface while not freaking out when plans don't go our way. Pause to read this book!"　　—Mike Robbins,
author of *Nothing Changes Until You Do*

"If you are like me, making a friendship with uncertainty can be daunting. Fortunately, Rachael O'Meara's new book is a practical tool kit for navigating and facilitating change. What I've learned from *Pause* changes everything."

—Barnet Bain,
director of *Milton's Secret*;
producer of *What Dreams May Come*;
author of *The Book of Doing and Being*

"If you've ever hit a wall, this book is for you. Rachael O'Meara knows—she's been there. *Pause* is an insightful and actionable road map for taking a moment to look inward, and making change that lasts."　　—Derek Sivers,
author of *Anything You Want*;
founder of CD Baby; TED speaker

"I can't recommend this book enough to those who are feeling stressed-out. As someone who turns off all screens with my family once a week for our weekly 'Technology Shabbat', I can promise you that bringing the ideas of *Pause* into your life will make your life better."　　—Tiffany Shlain,
Emmy-nominated filmmaker;
founder of The Webby Awards

"*Pause* gives you the permission you might have been looking for to take a break in your life or start on a new adventure. Rachael not only explains why it's important, but she also breaks down *how* you can do it."　　—Karen Henson Jones,
author of *Heart of Miracles*

Pause

Harnessing the Life-Changing
Power of Giving Yourself
a Break

Rachael O'Meara

A TarcherPerigee Book

tarcherperigee

An imprint of Penguin Random House LLC
375 Hudson Street
New York, New York 10014

Most TarcherPerigee books are available at special quantity discounts for bulk purchase for sales promotions, premiums, fund-raising, and educational needs. Special books or book excerpts also can be created to fit specific needs. For details, write: SpecialMarkets@penguinrandomhouse .com.

Pages 213–214: From *Letters to a Young Poet* by Rainer Maria Rilke, translated by M. D. Herter Norton. Copyright 1934, 1954 by W. W. Norton & Company, Inc., renewed © 1962, 1982 by M. D. Herter Norton. Used by permission of W. W. Norton & Company, Inc.

Library of Congress Cataloging-in-Publication Data
Names: O'Meara, Rachael, author.
Title: Pause : harnessing the life-changing power of giving yourself a break / Rachael O'Meara.
Description: New York : TarcherPerigee, [2017]
Identifiers: LCCN 2016046649 | ISBN 9780143129240 (paperback)
Subjects: LCSH: Burn out (Psychology)—Prevention. | Self-realization. | Stress management. | Change. | BISAC: BUSINESS & ECONOMICS / Motivational. | SELF-HELP / Personal Growth / Success.
Classification: LCC BF481 .O64 2017 | DDC 158—dc23 LC record available at https://lccn.loc.gov/2016046649

Printed in the United States of America
1 3 5 7 9 10 8 6 4 2

Book design by Katy Riegel

Pause for Ten Percent: Ten percent of all author royalties are donated to "Pause-some" nonprofits annually.

Dedication

For those who give themselves permission to pause.

For the transformers and those on their way to being and becoming.

*This book is about discovering for yourself what psychiatrist,
existentialist, and Holocaust survivor Viktor Frankl stated so clearly:*

Between stimulus and response there is a space.
In that space is our power to choose our response.
In our response lies our growth and our freedom.

In that space is the power of pause.

Contents

The wisdom is in the pause.

—ALICE WALKER

Foreword

PAUSE. The very word makes me take a deep breath.

How often do we feel like we are on fast-forward, just going through the motions? We may have a vague sense that we are off purpose—as if we've lost track of our dreams. Sometimes the way we're living just isn't bringing us the joy and satisfaction we desire.

If you want to get back in touch with what matters to you, take a breath or a prolonged break and be sure to get the most out of it. In *Pause*, Rachael O'Meara provides a menu of options richly illustrated to inspire you, whether you are taking a pause of a few minutes or a few months. She guides you with insight gleaned from her years of dedication to her own awakening and personal development.

Rachael defines a pause as any intentional shift in behavior that allows you the space to experience a mental shift in attitude, thoughts, or emotions that otherwise wouldn't have occurred. She shows us how to give ourselves permission to check in with ourselves, to step back, and listen to a self we so often overlook. This allows us to reorient and to pursue what it is we truly desire deep inside. By pausing, we begin to sense some of the subtle messages that tune us in to what we truly feel. We recognize long-buried desires. Better yet, we begin to sense how to meet those desires and chart a different course—before we burn out or find ourselves frantically spinning our wheels, going nowhere fast. Pausing takes us out of autopilot so we can stop going through the motions or feeling like we are sleepwalking through our lives. And if we are already burned out, dissatisfied, unfulfilled, going nowhere, or feeling stuck, pausing allows us to realign with our inner self and adjust our course toward fulfillment, satisfaction, and enjoyment of our lives.

Rachael's life could be defined by *Pause*. Ever since I've known her, she's been pushing the envelope, constantly learning and growing, taking a course, challenging herself, attending another conference, or building her leadership skills. I've had the pleasure of seeing her pause and shift again and again. She is consistently learning to live with greater mindfulness, consciously developing her emotional intelligence to be in touch with herself and with others. She is always looking to expand her ability to pause, check in with herself, and be guided by her inner feelings—to tune in to her deeper desires in each moment of her life. Rachael practices what she preaches, and in this book she delivers hard-won wisdom that anyone can learn from.

In my work, I've had occasion to study exceptional people and how they succeed at work, in relationships, self-development, and community service. What we've discovered is that people who live great lives are masters of pausing, checking inside to notice their deeper yearnings and operating according to their own values and principles. They're engaging in life to fulfill their yearning, not just their earning. They learned and oriented their behavior toward greater fulfillment. It was not just one pause—they were choosing to pause as a way of living, consistently listening to their inner voice.

This kind of pausing means being conscious, awake, in touch with our heart, our deeper feelings, the longings of our soul, and then guiding our actions by them.

You'll find a plethora of ways to pause in this book—big pauses, little ones, momentary ones, life-changing leaps, and small adjustments that bring big results.

Pausing is like tuning up before an orchestra concert so that you play at your best and be in harmony with life. Rachael illustrates her points with true life stories, exercises, research, and encouragement. She makes it all feel possible. You come away with the feeling of *I can do this!* We can live our lives as an adventure, always creating fresh experiences, with new ways to learn and grow, become our best, and provide our greatest service.

And by the way, you don't have to go to a cave in the Himalayas (unless that's your thing). You probably don't need to change your career or end a relationship—pausing doesn't need to start with a life shift. Life is happening moment by moment. Pausing helps you orient to fulfilling ways of being in these moments. And when you get off course, you can take a pause to help you look inside and realign.

Rachael talks about sleepers, those of us sleepwalking through our lives, going through the motions, living out some pattern or formula we were told was the way to live. Pausing gives us ways to wake up and live more consciously, to live mindfully and full of heart. Sleepers have unsatisfied longing, a feeling that something isn't quite right. They are burned out or itching to get away or anxious to do something different. These are all indicators of what our research identified as unfulfilled yearning—those deep longings we all have to exist, to see and be seen, to love and be loved, to be known, to be understood, to matter, to make a difference, to learn, grow, experience, express, create, or be part of something greater than ourselves. These are the unfulfilled yearnings that are crying out to be addressed. And if we don't pause, pay attention, look beneath the upset, and unlock the dissatisfaction, we won't discover what it is that's been trying to get our attention. Like a little kid tugging at our pant leg, our inner self is trying to get us to pay attention to our soul's longing. Get off of autopilot, go underneath the busyness—pause. Read on and get in touch with yourself, and become the self you most yearn to become.

JUDITH WRIGHT, PHD
Author of Transformed! The Science of Spectacular
Living, The Heart of the Fight, The Soft Addiction
Solution, *and* The One Decision*; founder, Wright
Foundation for Human Potential; professor, Wright Graduate
University for the Realization of Human Potential*

Introduction

Four years ago, I was working at Google, in a job that was the envy of all my friends as a customer support manager. But really, I was miserable. All I could think about was work. I would be at friends' houses, and while everyone else was engaged in conversation, I was in my own world, two feet away, lost in my e-mails and worries.

I decided I'd hit my limit. I was the definition of a corporate burnout. I had set off a self-inflicted mental panic and was spinning out of control. My negative self-talk wasn't healthy or sustainable, and I had received warnings from supervisors about my recent poor performance. I was too young to retire, but I couldn't continue on this way. Something had to give.

Luckily, before I self-destructed entirely, I realized that I had to take a meaningful look at my life—what I call a *pause*. Fortunately, Google is one of 15 percent of global companies that offer an unpaid leave of absence to certain employees.[1] I removed myself from my usual day-to-day life—which had become a deep rut—to tune in to what aligned with what felt right, how I could take responsibility to change it, and engage in new ways of thinking, doing, and being. I was learning how to be more present, a skill I had never understood before.

Almost everyone will encounter a time in his or her life when a pause is necessary. The good news is *everyone, including you, can pause.*

I was one of the incredibly lucky few to work at a company that allows for unpaid (or paid) leaves of absence. But a worthwhile pause experience does not necessitate a break from work life. Pausing isn't tied to any amount of time. It's about the quality of how that time is spent. I define a pause as any intentional shift in behavior that allows you space to experience a mental shift in attitude, thoughts, or emotions that otherwise wouldn't have occurred.

Pausing can be as simple as a five-minute walk outside, or a day spent unplugged from digital devices. A pause is about taking a time-out to create the space for your inner voice to be heard and to align your actions with that voice in order to lead a more meaningful, fulfilled life. Pausing offers you a chance to remember what "lights you up," and allows you to identify your yearnings, shift your limiting beliefs, recognize and better understand what's called "amygdala hijacks," and discover how your relationships with others affect you.

In this book you will learn how you can create your own "pause plan," regardless of your resources, and how psychology-based research proves that pausing can enhance your emotional intelligence and ability to act, feel, and communicate authentically and responsibly. You will also learn from other people's stories—from some whose pause was motivated by being laid off from a job to others who managed to create the

time and space to pause while continuing their daily lives otherwise as is. You will learn to recognize the signs that you
need to pause, how to prepare for one, the types of pauses
possible, tips for creating a meaningful experience, and how
to return to everyday life postpause with mental clarity and
maintain your "pause mindset" long afterward. You'll learn to
tune in to your inner voice to avoid perpetual "monkey
mind." (This is the mindless chatter that distracts us from the
real matters at hand.)

This book is for you if you have felt disconnected, caught
up in the whirlwind of life, and unable to keep your feet
firmly on the ground. Pausing was such a profound experience that I must share my story. I am here to help you give
yourself permission to take a pause and lead a more fulfilled
and satisfying life. There are ways we can avoid allowing ourselves to become burned out as quickly and often as we do.
There is a way to turn the tide. It is the power of pause.

Chapter 1

Training for Peak Performance

*To be yourself in a world
that is constantly trying to make you something
else is the greatest accomplishment.*

—RALPH WALDO EMERSON

I BEGAN MY BUSINESS CAREER in the fall of 1995. For three years I lived right across from beautiful, historic Prospect Park in Windsor Terrace, Brooklyn. Every morning I commuted one hour into Midtown Manhattan. There the skyscrapers kissed the sky and tourists craned their necks to see how far a building climbed. My office was housed at the same address as Radio City Music Hall, the same place that the leggy Rockettes called home. Next door was Rockefeller Center and my favorite spectacle, the Rockefeller Center ice skating rink. My lunch hours were filled watching skaters glide by the golden statues. I felt injected with inspiration. I had launched myself into the orbit of international business. I dwelled in the heart of New York City, at the age of twenty-three. On all counts, I had "made it."

Despite this success, I felt like something was lacking in my daily routine. Every night I came home feeling unfulfilled. At a certain point, the routine of riding the F train, stepping into my office, spending weekends partying away my hard-earned cash, and coming home to an apartment full of roommates didn't seem all that rewarding. I felt like I had more I was meant to do. Something was missing.

The following spring, I signed myself up for a rowing club, a lifelong passion and sport I had excelled at before moving to New York. I found myself gunning for the national team, rowing daily in the quiet dawn for the New York Athletic Club. We'd meet the sun and watch the morning sky unfold in velvet stripes of pinks and yellows. Without even knowing it, I found my first pause in rowing. It happened between every stroke, in between breaths, and before, during, and after my workout. As a rower, I paused all the time. Rowing taught me how to be present, no matter what was in store for me. I held on to that feeling throughout my day, excited to do it all over again the next morning.

Falling back in love with rowing helped me realize that I wanted more out of my working life. I wanted to feel the same passion in the office. I realized I longed to join the burgeoning Internet industry and found a new job at a promising start-up called DoubleClick.

Fast-forward a few years. Once again, I found myself longing for more. I transferred to the San Francisco DoubleClick office after ten years in New York City. It was time for a change. I was fixated on the city's beauty, lifestyle, and technology hub. Three years later, Google acquired the company. All seemed well on both the career and the personal front. I met my boyfriend Doug nine months after I moved to San Francisco. A few months later I bonded with a small group of girlfriends from a women's leadership class who became lifelong allies. My success was now bicoastal. I felt grateful and content to live the life I had created.

My lifestyle continued this way for five years. But I was hungry for a new challenge at work. Like so many other newly minted MBAs, I wanted to manage people. I wanted to make a difference in not just the work I was doing, but in other people's lives. I decided to go after a job to manage a customer support team working with advertisers on one of the company's flagship products.

Hitting a Wall

After six months leading a customer support team that ranged in size from four to eleven people, I hit a wall in my performance. I received feedback from my new supervisor that I wasn't up to par and needed to be a better communicator, listener, and manager. I began to question my decision to take on an unfamiliar role. I was confused about what success looked like at my job. For the first time in my corporate career I was receiving consistent feedback that my performance was poor and that I needed to change in order to be successful at Google.

What had happened to me? After all my success, what had gone wrong? After two years at Google, was it time to leave? How did I go from being a confident, successful woman, achieving promotions and praise year after year, to what felt like a floundering failure? Around this time, I began experiencing relationship trouble with Doug, who was now my boyfriend of five years. Neither of us could seem to move forward in our relationship. We were stuck.

Call it a midlife crisis of sorts, but I was miserable, lackluster, and beaten on all counts. I didn't know where to turn, but I knew I was in trouble. I felt a complete lack of purpose or direction. I felt unmotivated at work and, on some level, in my personal life. Commitment seemed to be my stumbling block, whether it was committing to one specific career ladder or to creating a successful relationship with my boyfriend.

I was burned out from trying so hard in this new and challenging capacity. I took all the Google training sessions I could, but I was told I lacked strong communication skills and "executive presence." I wasn't driving results for our team projects as much as I should. I missed the mark on executing ideas and contributing to our larger management team. I received the feedback over the course of several months, with no marked improvement.

I was drowning in my own negative self-talk. I wasn't sure I'd ever meet expectations in the eyes of my managers. I felt as stuck at work as I did in my personal relationship. I needed to bring my team to the next level. I longed to provide direct and constructive feedback to my team. I didn't know how to do it. I felt like a failure. It wasn't unusual for me to leave work at night only to cry during my dinner conversations with Doug.

My mental state was a mess. My confidence evaporated a little more every day. I felt like my wheels were spinning. I knew that a change was inevitable. My boss conveyed this to me one spring morning. Perplexed and tired, I sat there with Margaret in our cold, sterile conference room. She explained to me how things "just weren't working out" despite numerous reviews to assess what needed to change in my demeanor, work, and effort. What I heard was, "Rachael, you are a miserable failure. Please exit the building immediately."

Margaret gave me a choice that day. I could find a new role before things got ugly, or I could stay in the position and continue to receive subpar performance reviews, likely until I was let go. I would receive a ninety-day improvement plan intended to get me back on track. Both seemed like unfortunate options. I left the room diminished. I felt misunderstood. It certainly wasn't for a lack of effort or desire that things weren't working out well. I had to report back with a plan the following week. How could I possibly make any decision in my frenzied mental state?

I left work that day depressed and bewildered as to how I'd gotten so off track. Before my role as a support manager, I had been told I was a high performer. How had I gotten so bad at my job? How had things gone so terribly wrong despite my efforts to be successful? Peddling home that Friday, I wondered if I should quit everything that Monday. I asked myself if I should start job-hunting over the weekend. Should I aim for a new job at Google with my tarnished credibility and bruised ego? I went back and forth, stoplight by stoplight, flipping between these two options. I was not in a healthy mental position to look for a new job, regardless of what company or position it was. The voice inside me knew that much. Something needed to change, but I didn't know what.

That Saturday, I Skyped with two of my best girlfriends, Kathleen and Sue. As I explained my debacle, I pondered something out loud. "Google has a sabbatical program," I told them. "Maybe I should take that."

On the other end, there was silence. I didn't know if there was a delay in the video streaming or if the silence was deliberate. Almost in unison, my friends agreed that was a great idea. Sue filled my head with suggestions to come visit her, hang out on the beach, go to Europe, and indulge in some well-deserved downtime. She convinced me that these were all ideas worth exploring.

"You know, Rach, my old boss, who I consider a mentor,

once asked me what I would do if I knew I wasn't going to fail," Sue said.

"I definitely wouldn't be in this job!" I laughed back.

Sue explained. "It means you shouldn't worry about failing. Let yourself figure out what to do, knowing that whatever you decide, failure won't be considered failure unless you think of it like that."

I sat in silence, absorbing her insightful feedback.

While my friends encouraged me not to think of my job as a failure, the thought of taking a leave of absence lingered. Though it required approval from management, and I wouldn't get paid, I could keep my benefits. This was the permission slip I was waiting for. I could reboot and regroup on next steps.

Time to Take a Pause

I spent the rest of my weekend daydreaming about my plan. Ninety days! I felt a sense of duty to reclaim myself. I had a renewed sense of purpose. I could shift gears and find a new role at Google or elsewhere. I thought about the tempting urge to "check out" and do absolutely nothing. I could take my time to figure out what I really wanted to do, and then go do it. I could rebuild my confidence that I so desperately needed to find again. Maybe I'd travel. It all seemed possible, and for the first time in weeks I was smiling. I had the financial resources to enjoy unpaid leave thanks to my frugal upbringing and those scrappy days living on meager wages in Brooklyn. I had a decent amount of cash stashed away for a rainy day. This was my rainy day.

All I needed was my supervisor, Margaret, to give me the

green light. I pitched my idea clearly and with earnest openness. "I think the best thing for me to do at this point is to
apply for an extended leave. I've researched Google's policy on
leaves of absence and think this is the best option for me. I feel
too burned out to make any sound career decisions. I need to
regroup. I'd like your approval to take a ninety-day unpaid
break from Google."

She promised to talk to her managers and make sure everyone was on board with the plan. She also threw out her terms.
We agreed that I wouldn't return to my current role. I'd spend
the next six weeks looking for my replacement, training him
or her, and wrapping up my projects. My new adventure—my
new life—would begin June first.

I felt like a euphoric schoolgirl, scheming my plan for summer. The idea of having ninety days to figure out my next big
career move was a godsend. I wasn't ready for anything else
mentally, physically, or emotionally.

I knew there was something bigger and better for me
ahead. I had a spring in my step. I had a plan, even though I
had no idea what to plan. I would no longer be miserable or
stuck in my negative thought patterns. I was happy again, for
the first time in as long as I could remember. I was on my way
to saying good-bye to struggle, failure, and disappointment.

Practice of Pause Moments:
Chapter 1

At the end of each chapter there is a section that includes questions and exercises called "Practice of Pause Moments." I suggest writing out your responses and insights. Designate a

journal (or what I call a *pausebook*) for your ongoing insights that emerge from pausing.

Follow Your Breath

I recommend practicing this exercise before each chapter's Practice of Pause Moments. I suggest making this part of your daily routine. Experiment with what timing works for you. Use this practice of pause so you can have an easy, intuitive way to shift your state of being. Bring it into your life in whatever way works: before you get up in the morning, while you eat your breakfast, or in the car. It is one of the most powerful tools you can use to create a moment of pause.

Find a comfortable and quiet place where you can focus and sit down. If you are in a chair, sit up straight with your spine straight and both feet rooted firmly on the ground. If you are on the ground, sit cross-legged or on a pillow with your pelvis raised slightly higher than your legs.

1. Close your eyes and focus solely on your breath.
2. Take a deep, relaxing breath. Inhale through your nose for a count of five seconds. Exhale through your mouth, and count to seven in a steady rhythm. Do this for five breaths. Place your hand over your belly if you want to focus more on it as you feel your diaphragm rise and fall.
3. After the first five breaths, on your next inhale say to yourself or out loud, "I am present."
4. Inhale. On your next exhale say to yourself or out loud, "I listen to my inner voice to truly know what's best for me."

5. For the next thirty seconds focus on your breathing, alternating these two phrases. Don't worry about how long it takes. If you feel your body and mind settle in and relax, you'll know you've done enough. If you are restless, simply return to your breath counting. Refrain from judgment; simply notice your breath.

6. Notice your body and the sensations or emotions that arise. In your journal write down your observations or what you experienced. Aim to write nonstop for three to five minutes.

What would you do if you chose the power to pause for:

- A few minutes?
- An hour?
- A day?
- Any amount of time?

Imagine how you would feel in each example.

How else would you want to pause? For example, do you want to spend time with a specific person or group? Would you learn a new skill or participate in your favorite hobby? Would you choose to connect with someone to shift a relationship? What would be significant for you that you would want to begin? Whatever you choose it can be unique and meaningful because it is for you. This is your first step in creating your own practice of pausing.

Chapter 2

Five Signs You Need a Pause

Excellence is never an accident. It is always the result of high intention,
sincere effort, and intelligent execution; it represents the wise choice of
many alternatives—choice, not chance, determines your destiny.

—ARISTOTLE

YOU MAY START OUT, like I did, in a relatively content place.
You hold a position in life—whether it is a specific occupation
or a family role like a primary caretaker. You enjoy many aspects of your life. Your career is in a good place. You are financially stable and have a well-paying job. You may even be
in a relationship that you adore and enjoy. Your family is supportive, caring, and nurturing at least some, if not all, of the
time. On all counts you are successful and content with everything you've accomplished up until now. In other words,
you've made it.

The Wake-Up Call

However, for some reason, things aren't sitting well lately.
Restlessness sets in. You feel drained several times throughout

the day. Cracks are beginning to appear around your seemingly comfortable life. You realize your rock-solid foundation maybe is not so rock solid. Your current situation has been what the external world considers successful, but perhaps you forgot about your own satisfaction and fulfillment. You were too busy going for the next thing. Maybe you felt obligated to please others. Maybe material gain was your primary goal, or at least one of your top motivators.

I invite you to take a deep breath (a pause, if you will). Ask yourself, "What is going on with me internally and emotionally? Is it matching what is happening externally in my environment?" In other words, are you aligned? What does that do for your sense of spirit? Maybe you aren't feeling as successful as you once used to, or you lack the motivation you once had. It's what some may call a rut.

As I began to consider my own pause, I realized there were five major signs or clues that screamed, "Danger ahead. Proceed with caution." Initially I ignored every one. But each sign served a little more to tell me I needed to change. I needed a pause. If even one of these signs has shown up for you, congratulations! You just received one of life's perfectly well-timed wake-up calls to assess your own environment and correct your course.

Sign 1:
You Used to Love Your Job; Now You Loathe It

In my early days as a manager, I came to work cheerful and excited. What problems would I solve? What challenge would I overcome? How could I leverage what I knew about our products and help clients meet their needs? When I took on my new support manager role, a lot of new and challenging responsibility came with it. Whatever skills I had gotten by with in the past were no longer cutting it as a manager. In the past, I was told I was an excellent communicator and presenter. Now I was told I needed executive presence and clear, concise messaging. I wasn't practicing good listening skills. As a result, I was often checked out in meetings. I had to direct my team to innovate on tools. We weren't moving fast enough, and we seemed to be stuck. Or rather, *I* wasn't moving fast enough, and *I* seemed to be stuck.

I was too stressed out, and I couldn't stop thinking about how poorly I was doing. I lost confidence. As the months progressed, I continued to focus on my negative thoughts. I began to believe them. I was in a downward spiral where negative thoughts fed on each other around the clock. This fueled negative actions, which led to more negative thoughts. The mental loop was in full effect. I was burning out fast. Nothing in my day-to-day reality had changed on the outside. On the inside, it was another story. I was a mess.

Do you no longer enjoy what you do despite having been excited and invested in your job previously? Does it feel like you are no longer fulfilled by what you do or you're experiencing burnout? If your responsibilities have not changed but suddenly the perception of your performance at work has deteriorated, clearly something isn't working. Taking a pause, or intentionally shifting your behavior, is one way you can help yourself enjoy what you do again.

Your not-so-positive career shift could be for any number of reasons. Eventually you experience at least one self-deprecating thought, which may spiral into many more before you know what happened. Thoughts like "I can't do this any-more" or "Why am I so bad at this job?" become the new norm and can no longer be ignored.

A Word on Burnout

Does any of this, commonly known as burnout, sound famil-iar? What causes burnout? When you deprive yourself of emotional and personal nourishment in the present moment, eventually burnout may become a serious side effect. What do I mean by that? Dr. Bob Wright, a well-known coach and educator, puts it in layman's terms. "Imagine you are a blood donor. You give blood regularly, but you never eat to replen-ish your reserves or receive blood transfusions from other do-nors. Over time you have less energy and no longer feel strong and healthy to supply blood. Physically and emotionally you feel tired, weak and drained. You literally bleed yourself dry by avoiding meeting your yearnings and engaging in life to feel emotionally nourished and satisfied."[1]

I am all for working hard, but it needs to be balanced with meeting your deeper hungers, called yearnings, while doing so (more on that in Sign 3). Maybe you connect one-on-one with someone and give or ask for a hug. Maybe you spend some time being 100 percent present with a loved one, child, or pet. Don't be afraid to be present emotionally, make mis-takes as you experiment, and really engage with others. All of this helps to avoid burnout. Instead of bleeding yourself dry, engage in what is meaningful for you.

Sign 2:
The Boss Tells You It's Not Working Out

There's nothing like being on the receiving end of this message. In my case, my boss told me she felt like a broken record giving me specific examples, time after time, of where I was failing. We had words about my lackluster performance on several occasions.

"You need to be a more effective communicator," Margaret would say matter-of-factly. "You need to stand behind your ideas with conviction." For her, it was a signal that I couldn't put a stake in the ground and that I was not a strong manager. In hindsight, I couldn't make decisions on account of my own self-doubt. I knew this couldn't continue if I wanted to succeed at work.

There were many occasions like this. They all added up. I got tips on *what* to improve, but I didn't know *how* to improve. Margaret tired of telling me all the ways I needed to step up my game. Eventually she summed it up well: "You're not a fit for this role."

Maybe you got a similar message from your supervisor. Many times this message comes with the proverbial pink slip and a personal escort from your desk to the closest exit. But it may appear as a subtle note in a performance review, a seemingly casual meeting with your boss, or feedback from someone who sees (or hears) the writing on the wall.

It is easy to be in denial, like I was, when you're not ready to accept something. Each time Margaret offered feedback, I shrugged it off as something only she noticed. Each occasion was a mini problem, and the reality was I wasn't resolving anything. I rationalized that Margaret couldn't see all the value I was providing. I was convinced that she simply "was mistaken" and didn't recognize all the terrific, incredible work and results to which I was contributing. My ego was having a blast feeding me stories. It was a case of "me versus them" and "they" had it all wrong.

Without taking a pause, I would have continued this pattern in any future job—or any area of life, for that matter. Pausing is a gift. When you can shift your behavior, your passions and strengths will emerge and help you align with a more suitable environment for you. If you consciously and objectively look at your situation, your awareness will deepen, and change is more likely to occur. Taking a pause is a prescriptive way to shift your mindset so you can move forward and find where you can thrive. Pausing is an opportunity to shift what isn't working for you and take personal responsibility, without jumping into the next activity, role, or job and repeating your pattern all over again.

Sign 3:
An Intervention Separates You from Your Work or Technology

Chances are you have access to the Internet at some point during the day. You can check updates on Facebook, tweet on Twitter, or browse your friends' photos to abandon on any social media site. You most likely engage with technology in some aspect for your work or personal life and, like most people nowadays, you might be getting a little too much "screen time." In other words, you may need a technology intervention.

In my case, this intervention was a necessary message. As I

embarked on my pause, Kathleen, my best friend from business school, agreed to join me on a three-day celebratory
kickoff. We were headed to the heart of wine country, Sonoma
County, California. She was in between jobs, on her own
pause. She was a typical New Yorker—brash and not one to
be shy with her opinions. She always told me her thoughts
straight up. As we left the hills of San Francisco and headed
northbound across the Golden Gate Bridge, Kathleen shared
her concerns for me.

"Rachael, you spend too much time with technology. You
seem somewhat obsessed. You need to disconnect more. Every time I see you, you are checking e-mail, working, or connected to the Internet. I don't think you should be so engrossed
in this behavior anymore."

I turned to her and calmly responded, "Is this my intervention?"

"Yes," she said sternly. "You need to unplug and get back
in touch with reality. How can you function if you're always
so plugged in all the time?"

Here I was on day one of my pause and I was staring at my
truth. I'd become so engaged with work and focusing on the
end goals, I'd forgotten what mattered. I was obsessed with
cleaning up my e-mail in-box, finishing reports, and pleasing
others instead of myself. I'd lost sight of being human and being present. I knew I went overboard sometimes—prioritizing
work over friends or family, working on weekends, and not
disengaging with a screen. Sadly, it was all true. My weekends
ended early on Sunday afternoons. I felt obligated to respond
to e-mails to anticipate any issues Monday morning. I wasn't
aware I had a choice to disengage. Instead, I felt like this behavior was normal and almost expected in my world.

You may not have such a literal intervention as I did. It

may be more subtle. For example, your partner may insinuate that you prefer cozying up to your devices instead of him or her. Doug never said that, but I'm sure he thought it several times as he competed for my attention while I permitted my devices to distract me way too often. Maybe your friends have grown to expect that you will answer work calls at social events or dinners (as their unsurprised expressions suggest).

However you receive your wake-up call, it is important to realize the motives underneath your actions. Why are you attached to a given device or application? In my case I realized that I wanted to fulfill my hunger to matter. Someone e-mailed or messaged me—hooray! Despite my failures on the job, these technology interactions were little signals to me that I did matter. I was placating my feelings through casual connections on social media sites and answering e-mails.

What I didn't know then was that I was shortchanging myself. I was using surface-level means to connect and feel "plugged in" with others to meet my deeper hungers, or *yearnings*. If you feel the urge to repeatedly check your messages, you may not be attuned to your yearnings. This is when you need an intervention, even if it is a self-directed one.

In their book *The Heart of the Fight*, Judith Wright, EdD, and Bob Wright, EdD, define yearnings as "adaptive mechanisms that initially developed for our survival."[2] The Wrights explain how every individual—all seven billion of us on the planet—is hardwired to yearn, and this is what drives us to relate, to bond, and to commune with others as well as to develop ourselves. Do you want to be safe? Or be seen? Do you yearn to be loved or to matter? Do you yearn to make a difference? These are a few universal hungers, or yearnings.

As humans, we are designed to yearn, and it happens throughout our lifetime.[3] Evolution rewards us: when we follow our yearnings, we get a flood of feel-good neurochemicals in our system.[4] In any given moment, we may have one of five primary emotions: fear, hurt, anger, sadness, or joy.[5] Our emotions are directly connected to our yearnings. The more in tune we are with how we feel, the more able we are to express our feelings and fulfill our yearnings. How many times have you wanted to say something or share how you feel, but decided it wasn't worth it, or didn't follow through? Every time you decide it's not worth it, you are, on some level, saying *you* aren't worth it.

This is why technology interventions are important. When we do not fulfill our yearnings, they surface in other ways, like checking social media to feel connected through technology. If you learn to discern surface wants (let me check my e-mail) from deeper yearnings (I want a hug) in any given moment, you can focus on fulfilling your underlying yearnings and feel more satisfied.[6] Our surface-level actions indicate our deeper yearnings. I'm all for social media, but when you substitute technology to feel more connected, an intervention can help get you back on track.

Where in your life are your yearnings being met, and where aren't they? If you had to intervene in a specific area of life to follow more yearnings, what would it be? By taking a closer look at where you are or are not meeting your yearnings, you can change your behavior so that you can make choices that lead to greater fulfillment and satisfaction in your life.

Sometimes it is difficult to identify what we yearn for if all we see or think about is on the surface. Pausing is one way you can raise your awareness and align with what your deeper yearnings are. If you're in need of an intervention, chances are you may be off track. A great way to uncover yearnings is to employ what Bob and Judith Wright call the "so that" test.[7]

Think of something that you want, like a vacation (or a pause). If you apply the "I want X so that . . ." format to this desire, you can uncover a new layer.

I want a vacation *so that* I can feel less stress.
I want to feel less stress *so that* I can relax and snorkel at the beach.
I want to snorkel at the beach *so that* I experience the thrill.
I want to feel the thrill of snorkeling *so that* I can feel alive.
I want to feel alive . . . I yearn to feel alive.

What do you yearn for? Are you using a surface action to placate your deeper yearning(s)?

Pausing to identify your yearnings is a great way to shift to align your surface-level actions with your deeper-rooted yearnings. It doesn't require an intervention; you can pause and identify your yearnings at any time to align with what really matters.

Here are just a few examples of universal yearnings:[8]

- To feel alive (to experience fully, to create, to express, to learn and grow)
- To be secure (to exist, to connect, to trust)

- To be loved (to love, to feel appreciated, to belong, to connect)
- To matter (to be valued, to contribute, to make a difference)

PAUSE STORY
Judith Wright

From Conscious Clinician to Transformational Educator

Judith Wright is one of my teachers, one of my mentors, and, more importantly, one of my heroes. She was a leader among leaders throughout high school and early on in her career in pioneering services for college students with disabilities not only to have access to higher education—which was groundbreaking at that time—but also to thrive and succeed in education and community life. As director of clinical programs for the Illinois Institute for the Study of Developmental Disabilities, she developed a new model of transdisciplinary service delivery and community support for families of children with developmental disabilities. She and her husband, Bob Wright, cofounded the nonprofit Wright Foundation for the Realization of Human Potential along with the Wright Graduate University, offering graduate certificates in social intelligence and emotional intelligence and master's and doctoral degrees in transformational leadership and transformational coaching.

Budget: Enough to cover gas and food and retreat fees

Duration: Weekends, at first; now one week a year and daily moments

Goal: Be conscious, alive, awake, and engaged in every moment; live life as a sacred journey

Trigger: While her clinical career challenged her intellectually, Judith felt that something was missing, that she wasn't tapping her intuition and deeper essence. She wanted to renew and reacquaint herself with her yearnings to feel alive, engaged, and fulfilled in life. She wanted to discover what mattered most while she stepped away from what was familiar to her.

Plan: Judith began pausing by taking one weekend a month on a personal retreat, driving off with her bicycle on the back of her car. From oak groves to lakesides, Judith spent her time exploring the local communities and sights. Her trips would often land her in the space that most renewed her soul— Mother Nature. She took long bike rides, wandered on nature walks, read inspirational books, listened to empowering music, and free-form journaled. She always paused in prayer or meditation. This practice helped her deepen her connection to her spirit and better know herself.

Judith minimized technology everywhere she went: no phones, laptops, or electronics (except for journaling) as a general rule. She continues this deep connecting today, pausing every morning to engage in a daily ritual she created to reflect her relationship to the divine and focus on the purpose for the day, and adding periodic stops throughout the day as she continues to look inward for inspiration and vision.

Judith's weekend retreats eventually became annual weeklong "spiritual pilgrimages," a tradition she has kept going since 1987. Initially, the plan was simple—she would explore and travel to the most sacred sites in the world, picking one location a year where she would learn about local spiritual traditions, meet spiritual leaders, and create and participate in mystical experiences. Soon word of her travels spread to others, and she extended an invitation to students of all faiths in the Wright Foundation learning community to join her in the internal and external journey. From well-known UNESCO World Heritage Sites to out-of-the-way local sites of worship, her students have met deeply dedicated spiritual practitioners, deepened their understanding of themselves through other faiths, and joined local communities to share meditation, chanting, praying, and learning for almost thirty years.

Impact: Today, Judith takes lots of pauses that she's tailored to work for the very fast-paced life she has created for herself. Pausing led her to subtle changes in thinking. She realized there was no "absolute" way to be or do anything, and that self-worth wasn't about what she was doing externally. "I'm aware of what I am feeling, what I yearn for, and what really matters to me, and I act on that," Judith says. "My life might look similar from the outside, but from the inside, it is very different. I love my life. I *feel* my life. Every day is fulfilling. I realize that satisfaction is available every moment if I choose it. I am increasingly guided by my inner compass and from spirit. Pausing helped me listen to my inner wisdom, and I continue to listen to it every day."

PRACTICE OF PAUSE ADVICE

Discover, follow, and express your yearnings.
One key to happiness has to do with developing the discipline to notice and express your deepest yearnings—to love and be loved, to matter, to connect, to make a difference. You can take action and connect to them in every moment.

Note that these are different from escapes or surface-level wants (Judith calls these "soft addictions"—those quick fixes and habits like impulse buying or constantly checking your e-mail that actually mute and numb rather than express our yearnings).[9] Truly heeding the call of *deeper* yearnings begins by tuning in to them.

Engage in activities and in ways of being, thinking, and feeling that meet your yearnings.
Engaging means to act on your yearnings. That can mean journaling, reading, listening to music, and participating in conscious activities, but it also means being present with the person who is in front of you, being aware of your feelings, being engaged in all aspects of your life, and taking risks to learn, grow, and develop.

Dedicate yourself to pausing as a way of life.
In addition to annual pilgrimages, for many years Judith took a one-day pause away from work per week, what she referred to as a Sabbath. As her life has expanded into more weekend trainings, research, writing, and fewer unstructured days, she has learned to keep a Sabbath of a few hours or minutes, if that's all that's possible, in the midst of hectic days. Rather than indulge in mind-numbing habits as a break from a thorny project or after a difficult conversation, Judith takes mini Sabbaths to read an inspiring short story, cross-country ski through the woods at sunset, or have an impromptu dance break with her husband. What is important isn't a fixed time frame but rather finding your own rhythm, heeding your own yearnings to pause, listening to your inner voice, and sensing your path more fully. If you can make a ritual out of this at whatever frequency and for

whatever amount of time works for you, pausing will help you reconnect with yourself and your yearnings.

> **Avoid an intervention.** Instead of settling for feeling unsatisfied, ask yourself, "What do I yearn for?" Express it and follow your urges to meet your yearning. Keep it limited to interacting and engaging with people, not devices.

Sign 4
A Major Life Event, Challenge, or Change Happens

If you recently had a major change in any area of life, this is a good time to reflect and evaluate the results. I consider a major life event one that shifts how you behave, express your emotions, or spend your time. It may be positive or negative. It could be a health diagnosis. Perhaps there is a relationship beginning or ending. It could be the loss or birth of a loved one. Is there concern or fear around a move, a family member, or a physical or mental health issue? It may be difficult to adjust to a new schedule or newly inherited responsibilities.

Change is inevitable, and pausing to assess your options or before your next move is a prime opportunity to choose wisely. Pausing is one way to allow yourself the space to evaluate your choices and align with what matters to you. It could be driven by your yearnings or what is most important. The point is, when you allow yourself the time to pause, even if it's for one breath, you create the opportunity for a new thought, emotion, yearning, or behavior to emerge. Pausing or shifting your behavior can have a profound effect on what follows.

Noticing Change in Seven Areas of Life

Ever wondered how one change can create ripples that affect all parts of your life? Alfred Adler is considered one of the top influential thought leaders of modern individual psychology. Among his many contributions (there are entire schools dedicated to teaching his practices), he created the concept of exploring situations in the main areas of life: work, social, and relationships.[10] Bob and Judith Wright expanded on this concept to include seven areas: body, self, family, career, relationships, community, and spirituality.

If I were to examine my initial situation and the changes to the different areas of my life that resulted from the intervention, here is what it would look like:

Situation: I had little to no boundaries at work and felt compelled to prioritize work at all times. When I worked I felt important.

Limiting Beliefs: I don't matter unless I'm working. I am not good enough unless I'm working.

Yearnings: To matter and feel connected and present with others (versus my devices).

Action: I could choose when and how to use technology, prioritize my personal relationships, and give them full attention whenever possible.

When I took this action, I saw the following changes in these seven main areas of life:

Body: I felt more relaxed and less stressed. I slept better and my body was rested.

Self: I was more comfortable knowing that my work felt manageable. I felt my sense of self was developing as I focused on my own satisfaction and how I worked, instead of looking outside of myself for this affirmation.

Family: I had more time for my family. I prioritized my family. I mattered in my family.

Work/Career: I had specific times to focus on work. I had worked with my manager on what boundaries worked best for me and my team.

Relationships: I was more present in my personal relationships. I felt happier and more connected.

Community: I felt more present with others. When I walked down the street, I smiled and said hello.

Spiritual: I felt more connected to my inner voice. I asked for guidance if I felt compelled to change my boundaries or in one-off situations.

Now think of a situation that you want to change. How do you envision your life differently in each of the areas above?

Regardless of what life event or challenge happens, it is an ideal opportunity to recalibrate and pause. You can tune inward and pay attention to your inner voice. Ask yourself, "What primary emotion am I feeling in this moment?" Too often the emotional reactions to change are underplayed or glossed over, especially if we think an emotion isn't "good" to express. It's often not the feelings that are the real issue; it's that we tend to avoid expressing those emotions we're not comfortable with. Many of us grew up in families that didn't encourage certain feelings like hurt or fear to be expressed (or tolerated). Other families hardly expressed any emotions at all. Whatever the case, it is important to pause, create the space to tune in to yourself, recognize whatever you are feeling, and honor it by expressing it. Feeling afraid or hurt? Tell someone how you are feeling. Not sure if you can share anything? Write it down in a journal (or your pausebook). Connect with someone you haven't talked to in a while to say hello and catch up. Feeling reactive or angry? Ask yourself what happened that made you so angry.

Take inventory of your last twelve to eighteen months. Did a significant event happen? Did it affect anyone else in your life? Choose to be in the present moment and express how it has affected you. Let it sink in without rushing off to the activity, event, or responsibility. Avoid going through the motions and getting on with life as if nothing had happened. Life is handing you an opportunity to recalibrate. It is a gift. *You* are a gift. If you have experienced a life change, maybe it's a gift in disguise, or an opportunity to embrace the experience, rather than avoid it, and express yourself.

Once you start to think about any life change as an opportunity or gift, look to understand the deeper meaning and how you can use it as an opportunity to do something different.

The time I spent away from Google was the biggest gift I ever gave myself. A bigger gift was how Margaret held me to her high standards. I needed to fail in order to grow and reach my fullest potential. This gift was greater than any vacation spot, any present, or anything money could buy. I was oblivious to it at the time. Later, I saw the situation objectively: Margaret was doing her job and asking for my best.

I thought more clearly during my pause. I took responsibility for my actions. I finally realized and accepted that I was responsible for the situation I'd created. All these circumstances—the burning out, the stress, the unwieldy relationship—had one thing in common: me.

Sign 5
A New Opportunity Reveals Itself

Is there an opportunity you're thinking about but hesitating to act on, like taking a big trip, changing careers, or starting a project? Life really is short. Why live in the future? A pause allows you to live in the present and make better choices. It is a time to check in with your emotions. Do you primarily feel fear, sadness, joy, anger, or hurt when you think about this opportunity? What yearnings are behind your motivation to seize it? You can create a pause to check in on a deeper level and evaluate.

The Obvious, Unmistakable Opportunity

Opportunities can present themselves in irresistible ways. Do any of these scenarios sound familiar? You receive a spontaneous invite for a weekend away with your friends. You have a sudden urge to travel somewhere you've always wanted to visit. You hear from a friend you haven't heard from in a while who suggests getting together. You may reflexively respond to any of these scenarios by saying, "I can't do that!" But quietly you start scheming. You ask yourself, "What if?"

When you start considering an opportunity, focus on the emotion that accompanies it. Feel it in your body. Often you will instinctively know or feel that it's the right thing to do. It is what you want to happen to move forward in your life.

When I was twenty-one, I was already planning my first extended pause soon after I was to graduate. I sat in the library, distracted by thoughts about my future. What was I going to do once I graduated in May? I had no idea. I didn't want to go back to school, at least not then. I remember asking myself, "If I could do one thing after I graduate, what would it be?"

I had wanted to go to France ever since I said my first *"Je m'appelle Rachelle."* I decided that maybe I'd try to work in Paris or live there. I had no idea how I would find the money or pull everything together, but I smiled every time I thought about it. It was the authentic answer to what I truly wanted to do. This was the first time I created my own pause, even if I didn't call it that at the time. I spent my summer waiting tables at Pizzeria Uno in Albany, and every penny I made went toward my trip. I bought my plane ticket to leave on October 9 and return nine months later. I even secured a permit that allowed me to work in France.

Everyone thought I was brave—and crazy. At my birthday party a few months before I left, my friends asked, "Who gets to do this?" I plucked gummy bears off the rim of my cake and said, "I guess I do. I have no idea what will happen, but I'm going to go." I was scared but I knew I had to put one foot in front of the other and trust my instinct.

That winter I spent an unforgettable nine months working in the French Alps. Mission accomplished. This was my obvious opportunity and I seized it.

The Contemplative Opportunity

Inevitably, doubts arise when things aren't right at work, at home, or in other areas of life, like relationships. Each one deserves its own quiet time for deeper thought. Perhaps you feel a change stirring. You may need to hear it a few more times, but it's there and often shows up as a question that crosses your mind:

"Is this the right place for me?"
"Is this what I really want?"
"What am I doing here?"
"Should I be spending time doing this?"
"Is this relationship making me happy?"

That last question is a doozy. I asked myself this question with Doug the last year we dated. I was constantly weighing the pros and cons. We loved each other but we weren't emotionally connected most of the time. He didn't want to try a lot of new things that I'd recently discovered, such as meditation. I was content in our relationship, but was I satisfied? For me, satisfaction was about expanding and feeling good about where I was headed. I didn't feel that. Was I settling for a level of happiness that felt good only occasionally? This question crept up again and again for me. I ignored it. I convinced myself I was happy. In reality, I was in denial.

If any of these questions come up for you, it's likely a sign to look closer at a situation. It's your wiser self telling you that you aren't happy in your relationship, you aren't in the right job, or you don't want to do what you're doing. This is what I call "the contemplative opportunity." It doesn't mean you need to make a drastic change; it means a pause, or a change in behavior, may help you get clear about your situation.

I asked each of these contemplative questions right before, during, and after my pause from Google. Each question had a surface-level answer, but as I began to look closer at my own situation and my level of happiness, I realized my answers were different the deeper I looked.

The High-Risk Opportunity

Time is ticking to make a somewhat risky plan. It sounds like a whisper in your ear: "Revisit me. I think you will enjoy this. Spend more time thinking about me." You can ignore it, fear it, or forget it. After all, it involves risk. It requires time, courage, or money, and you are uncertain you can handle it, let alone succeed.

What is your high-risk opportunity? Is it a lifelong dream or passion of yours? What's the reason you haven't done it yet? Is the fear of failure holding you back? Or is it because it's unfamiliar territory, outside of your comfort zone?

Taking a pause may be what's needed to find out how serious you are about setting course on a risky idea. By setting aside time to be with your plan, you create space without the distractions of everyday life. A weekend getaway or doing something outside of your routine is the perfect pause to learn more about it. It may be exactly what you need to figure out the first step to get there.

The Pause Paradox

Each one of these opportunities is a paradox. Is taking a pause really meant to be time spent to think? Or is it time to *stop* thinking so the wisdom and answers have ample room to surface? How often have you stressed out about a specific situation or were stuck in the decision-making process because you couldn't make up your mind? Overthinking can kill just about everything.

Taking a pause isn't so you can think more. It's to do the exact opposite. It's the perfect excuse to step away from your everyday life and not focus on what is ruling your thoughts. Without the time to step away, you don't have the opportunity to sit with the idea. Have you rushed into a decision only because you were obsessed with an idea? Would your plan change if you took a five-minute pause instead?

 The New Parent Pause

I am not a parent, nor do I imply I have parental experience, but I think about how pausing relates to parenthood. If you are a parent or primary caregiver, or you are soon to become one, congratulations! It is an incredible time in life, and an excellent opportunity to let emotions flow and express whatever you are feeling, whether it's joy, fear, or anything in between. It is also a major life change that brings a shift in emotions and behavior.

This is a physically and emotionally challenging time. Try to think of it as an opportunity not only to care for your child, but to tend to yourself in ways that you may not have thought of before. You are growing as a new parent right alongside your child. You will be busy taking care of your child. Remember to care for yourself, too. As flight attendants always advise: put your own oxygen mask on first, then tend to others. Use this time to practice alert, conscious presence. And don't skimp on parental leave—take the maximum time off whenever possible.

Evaluate Your Signs

Think about your experiences over the last year and whether your outlook, output, or surroundings have changed. If you find yourself in any of the situations in this chapter, you are a prime candidate for a pause.

Maybe you pause to create some space so that you can figure out what is the best next step for you. By allowing yourself the space and time to pause, and to do it with purpose, you are allowing yourself the freedom to be present. When you are present, you're in alignment with knowing what is best for you. You are choosing to take action by not taking action. This is your sacred pause with purpose.

Pausing can help you discover who you really are and what you are passionate about because you are present and in alignment with yourself. You aren't distracted. Rather, you are operating from your own presence and stillness. This can create the space in which to do what matters to you, bringing you more joy in your day-to-day life.

Do you think you are currently present and in alignment with your yearnings? Go one step further. Imagine how other people's lives are affected by your choices. Are you as present as you would like to be in your personal and professional life? Who else in your sphere of influence would benefit from what you learn by pausing?

Now that you recognize the different signs that are a good indicator for creating a pause, take the self-assessment below and see how many signs you may have already experienced. If even one sign is present, it may be time for your own pause.

Practice of Pause Self-Assessment

Put a "1" next to the following signs that you have experienced.

_____ You used to love your job; now you loathe it.

_____ Your boss tells you it's not working out (e.g., fires you, gives you a negative performance review, asks you to look for another role, etc.).

_____ A friend performs an intervention (e.g., tells you you're not present or you're too preoccupied with something else) to clue you in.

_____ You experience a major life shift or event.

_____ You come across an opportunity you want to explore.

_____ **Total Score**

Scoring Chart

0—Congratulations! You are living the career and life of your dreams. Celebrate in whatever way feels right for you, which may include a celebratory pause to reflect on what is working well and how to continue doing it.

1 or 2—If one of the signs happens to you, it's worthwhile to plan a pause. Plan a vacation in the next three months. Assess your time frame and what you'll do; there'll be more on this in chapter 5.

3 to 5—You have enough reasons to consider seriously dropping out of society, hiding under a rock, or taking a pause for as long as you can.

Practice of Pause Moments:
Chapter 2

What are your primary yearnings? Use the "so that" exercise to home in on what resonates with you.

What signs (including a possible burnout) have you experienced that might indicate you need a pause?

After taking the self-assessment quiz, what primary emotion do you feel: fear, hurt, anger, sadness, or joy?

Reflect on your self-assessment and write down any additional insights or thoughts in your journal or pausebook.

What did you learn about yourself from discovering your yearnings, thinking about signs to pause, and your self-assessment?

Chapter 3

Taking the Pause Plunge

Decision is a risk rooted in the courage of being free.

— PAUL TILLICH

CONGRATULATIONS ON TAKING (or considering taking) the pause plunge. You probably don't know how long or short it will be yet, and even if you do, take it in stride. Plans change, and so can your pause. It's easy to get sidetracked creating to-do lists or travel plans to exotic destinations. We all want to control our destiny. Why should pausing be any different from any other type of endeavor?

Well, while our brains want to remain in charge, it is important to remember that when you take a pause, the outcome is unknown. Part of the thrill of pausing is leaving yourself open to be surprised by what happens. It's human nature to get in front of any relevant issues to ensure a set outcome. Letting go of control is one of the hardest habits to break.

The good news is that by taking a pause, you do let go. A pause is about *surrendering*. Pausing allows for the possibilities of the unknown. Trust that your pause is in your best interest, even if you have no idea what the outcome will be or where you'll end up. Trust in knowing that whatever lies ahead will serve you. Stay in present time. That's a lot easier to say than do. Believe in your mission, and replenish yourself by switching off in some way. This deeper sense of trust is what some people call their inner voice. I think of it as my inner guidance system that moves me forward in ways that serve my best interest.

When I started my pause I had no idea what the outcome would be, but I had faith in my decision. All I knew was that as a result of working too much and going into my mental tailspin, I needed time to "be" and check out. During the month between receiving approval for my extended pause and leaving Google, I wondered how I would spend my time. I was scared to make too many plans. I didn't want to feel over-whelmed again. I wanted to leave room for plans to create themselves. If I filled up my time with too much doing, how would there be room for any magic to happen?

Beginning a pause requires a combination of courage, risk, and self-assurance. In *The Hero with a Thousand Faces*, Joseph Campbell tells us more. He informs us that part of any "hero's journey" is to go through a challenge, obstacle, or threat and come out on the other side stronger and changed for the better. After you've pursued a journey as the hero, perceptions change. You are no longer the same person you were before your experience. Having faced your fears head-on, you return with new ideas, experiences, and lessons that allow you to grow. Through the act of pausing, you become the hero of your journey. That journey is an act of courage.

A pause means embarking on your own hero's or heroine's journey. As Campbell wrote, it is about facing the unknown. "A hero ventures forth from the world of common day into a region of supernatural wonder: fabulous forces are there encountered and a decisive victory is won: the hero comes back from this mysterious adventure with the power to bestow boons on his fellow man."[1]

Courage to Pause

German existentialist philosopher Paul Tillich wrote *The Courage to Be* in 1952; in this book he questions what it means to exist as a finite being. He introduces the concept that all anxiety is part of the human condition and implies that courage *is* being.[2] Not to get too existential on you, but courage is also pausing, and it's required for the decision to take the leap of faith in the actual act. It's a step toward finding the next bread crumb to follow or door to walk through. *Courage* is defined as "the ability to do something that you know is difficult or dangerous."[3] Part of what's gained in the pause process *is* courage. Pausing means being okay knowing you're uncertain of an outcome, letting go of control, or surrendering to the present moment. Each one is a tremendous act of courage.

I felt a tinge of fear every time I explained why I was pausing to curious people who asked me. I accepted it, like most uncomfortable feelings, but it didn't mean I stopped worrying. My biggest fear around my pause was that I would discover a side of me that I had ignored for far too long. What if I figured out I was not in the right job or career? I didn't want to think about how much energy or time I had spent convincing myself I was passionate about my job and technology.

What if I realized I was miserable? What if I didn't like myself? I felt hesitant to discover any of it. I didn't let myself feel my terror. I skimmed over it and refused to acknowledge it. I didn't realize it at the time, but this was exactly how I was supposed to feel. Since I was out of my comfort zone it was a normal reaction. I had to face the ignored and stuffed-down emotional pain I previously was unwilling to look at. It was like my body was an emotional safety-deposit box, holding emotions I didn't want to feel under lock and key indefinitely. I didn't realize that expressing them was important and would help me heal.

I had the same feeling when I began to write this book. My fear sat in the pit of my stomach. I questioned if I could do it and wondered if I would fail. Writing required more introspection and effort on my part. Fear of the unknown lurked in the shadows of my thoughts and actions.

I knew that worrying about what I would do postpause, without knowing any details, was pointless. Every time I started thinking about the future, it meant I was no longer present. I needed to face my biggest fear, the unknown, and trust that I was okay in it. I accepted the fact that whatever was on the other side of my three-month pause would be worth the risk. The reward of being more aligned and fulfilled was worth the price of the unknown, even if it meant discovering who I was, and who I wasn't, and facing it head-on. Courage would see me through.

Most of us do not live day in and day out free and fearless. According to G. M. Durst, approximately 70 percent of the population works to negotiate belonging and expression.[4] They live in conformity, not venturing beyond the norms of society and culture. They go to the school that makes sense, do what others expect or tell them to do, have a conventional career path, and don't question assumptions about their lifestyle, family, belief systems, or whatever is expected.

Austrian psychiatrist and Holocaust survivor Viktor Frankl reminds us, "What is to give light must endure burning."[5] I interpret "burning" to mean facing your own fears and having the courage to discover your true self and move beyond conformity. Frankl believed that people are primarily driven by "striving to find meaning in one's life," and that it is the sense of meaning that enables people to face their fears and overcome painful experiences. In Frankl's words, I was willing to face who I really was, and "burn" my fears, in order to develop a stronger sense of self.

What fear is in you, or in your life? Are you afraid of quitting, staying, or loss of control? A pause can help you discover who you can become and provides an opportunity to courageously embrace your fear and look at what is and isn't working for you. It can go way beyond finding a new job. It can be a way to heal and not rush off to the next thing with wounds exposed. Pausing is one way to give yourself permission to deeply connect with yourself, including feeling and expressing emotions, in ways you had not thought possible. This was true in my case, unbeknownst to me.

So, what does one do when plunging into the unknown? Where does one begin? Knowing you are stepping into the unknown, I've created three steps to help navigate your path. With a little guidance, my hope is that you harness your courage and take a leap of faith.

Three Steps to Taking the Pause Plunge

Figuring out how to structure a pause can be daunting. Planning a pause means planning in broad strokes. You'll still leave room for life to get in the way. You can set yourself up for success by strategizing how and what you plan to do in the big-picture kind of way.

Three Steps to Planning

1. Write your rough draft.
2. Set your intention.
3. Create your plan.

Step 1: Write Your Rough Draft

I heard Brené Brown speak on her *Rising Strong* book tour at the 2015 Google women's employee conference in Chicago. She introduced us to one of her core concepts: writing down your "sucky first draft" (although she used a different adjective!), or SFD. The idea came from Anne Lamott's insightful book *Bird by Bird*. Writing your story and ideas down, no matter how messy, ugly, or imperfect they are, is the first step to fostering awareness. It isn't something you need to share with others. Brown calls it the "first version that your child-like self can write."[6] She suggests we keep it to six bottom-line bullet points as we consider our whole selves and unfiltered stories: the story I'm making up, my emotions, my body, my thinking, my beliefs, my actions.

Your SFD can also spark ideas for your pause plan, or a way to set your intentions for your pause. Write down whatever you feel like, and give yourself full permission to express, write, and capture what your mind has to say. It doesn't have to be a sweeping, detailed narrative. It can be a few bullet points, a Post-it Note–sized paragraph, or a journal entry. Brown reminds us that our goal is wholeheartedness. That is the magic of an SFD.

I see the SFD as a critical step in identifying your limiting beliefs, acknowledging your fears, and creating intention and a plan for your pause. By creating this rough draft, you acknowledge your story and beliefs. You glean insights on how you want to spend your time (or not spend it), what your yearnings might be, and what actions you want to take (or not take). It allows you to "clear out" the thoughts you currently have and enter into the right frame of mind to create a plan for your pause.

How do you know if you are in the "right" frame of mind? If you convince yourself that you aren't ready to plan, remember this is often a default way of thinking and you can choose to shift it. Your limiting beliefs may be getting in the way of planning. Notice your attitude. Are you curious about what a successful pause plan looks like? Or, are you convinced it is what it is and maybe this is all a big waste of time? One way to support yourself, whether it is writing your SFD or any endeavor you take on, is to activate your growth mindset.

 ### Adopt a Growth Mindset

Do you have a fixed mindset or a growth mindset? Carol Dweck, PhD, a Stanford University researcher and professor, is one of the primary thought leaders and researchers on growth mindset. In her groundbreaking book *Mindset: The New Psychology of Success*, Dweck defines growth mindset as a "mental attitude that sees challenges as exciting rather than threatening."[7] Individuals with a growth mindset are those who tend to "just go for it." They look at an opportunity as something they can learn and grow from, even if they fail. Dweck believes that growth mindset is critical for anyone looking to be a good leader or learner. Those who have a growth mindset tend to be more curious, while those who are the opposite, with a more fixed mindset, are preoccupied with looking smart.

Each of us is capable of having a growth mindset when we set out to learn something new, but it is a choice we must make deliberately. Growth mindsets help us stay curious. For anyone daunted by a particular challenge, remember that those who adopt a growth mindset have a better chance to learn and grow than if they were not in that state of mind.

Keeping a growth mindset assures us that we never stop developing and that we are limitless when it comes to harnessing our potential. The only limit we have to our own intelligence, skills, or awareness is the cap we put on them for ourselves. Pausing to learn something new allows you to make a choice to adopt a growth mindset. It reminds you to stay out of your comfort zone and take on new challenges, whether it is increasing your knowledge base or your facility for emotional intelligence. Part of adopting a growth mindset means that you can anticipate triggers and blocks so that, when they happen, you can move through them, instead of giving up and retreating because you are blocked. By maintaining a growth mindset, you can continue to grow, learn, and pause instead of giving up.

Step 2: Set Your Intention

Setting intention is an easy way to tap into what you really want. Intention, or a determination to act in a certain way, adds meaning to your actions and helps you focus on a specific outcome. Intention is about envisioning what you want and going for it. Ask yourself, "What do I want to get out of this moment, afternoon, day, or pause?" If you're used to setting intentions, congratulations. You are on your way to a successful pause. Please note, intention setting is different from goal setting. Goals are specific, measurable, and timely outcomes. A goal is losing ten pounds in two months, learning Japanese this year, or having at least one date night a week. Goals are good motivators to act, but *how* you act is intention.

By setting intention, you create a vision for how you want to be and how you want to feel while pausing. Setting intentions before, during, and after your pause matters. For any successful pause, intention is not so much about what you do as it is about how you show up and what possibility arises in your new space—whether it's a day without screens, starting a new hobby, or going away for a long weekend.

Here are some examples of intention:

- Before you get out of bed, intend to be fully present with everyone you interact with.
- When you leave home, intend to spend quality time with your partner, a good friend, or family when you return.
- Before you start your car, intend to have a relaxing ride to work.
- Before you enter your place of employment, intend to show up in a calm state by taking six deep breaths.
- Intend to meet, smile, and speak with three strangers before noon.

Keep a pause journal or "pausebook" and write down your rough draft, or SFD. It becomes proof of your own talents, intentions, and capabilities during and after your pause that you can review and reflect upon. When I paused from Google, I didn't know about SFDs, so I didn't write one. Instead, I bought a five-by-seven-inch pink spiral notebook and called it my "career journal" to capture all my notes and insights from others. It was the validation I needed to see, documenting my capabilities.

Using Journaling As a Power Tool

When you journal, you empower yourself. Think of it as your personal power tool. The physical act of writing has a neurological effect on the brain. As Henriette Anne Klauser explains in *Write It Down, Make It Happen*, writing stimulates a bunch of cells in the brain called the "reticular activating system," or RAS, which in turn signals the cerebral cortex to wake up and pay attention.[8] There is also research concluding that journaling for as little as two minutes on two consecutive days about an emotionally significant event improves mood and well-being.[9] When you write down your intentions, insights, and observations on your emotional experiences along with your ideas about pausing, it can help you reflect on what changes to make over time. New ideas literally emerge from the paper—possibly ones you have not seen before.

Identify Your Strengths

Do you know what you are good at? Do others compliment you on what you are good at? It's important to take inventory of your strengths. The more you know where you excel naturally, the easier it is to see what isn't working and adjust.

According to a 2015 study of one thousand working men and women in the United States, the first step to finding happiness at work is strength awareness.[10] "Strengths alignment" occurs when a person can express signature strengths in his or her tasks at work. In fact, 79 percent of those surveyed who have the opportunity to do what they do best each day feel like they are making a difference and that their work is appreciated. This is the opposite of what we thought a decade ago, when 63 percent of us thought we would grow most by fixing our weaknesses. Turns out we grow more when we focus on our strengths. We also do better when we connect with our character strengths, such as being curious, and use them at work. This leads to on-the-job "flourishing," says strength pioneer and leader of the study Michelle McQuaid. McQuaid has a free, online one-week strength challenge anyone can try.[11]

I knew if I used my pause time to identify my strengths, I would learn more about myself and apply it to my career. I wanted my next job to leverage my strengths, no matter what I chose. I created an intentional mindset to understand my strengths and take on a role that would harness them. I also found my notes from a training course I'd taken a few years before using a book by Tom Rath called *StrengthsFinder 2.0*. I reviewed my top five strengths from my self-assessment to give me additional insight and perspective. (More on this in chapter 10.)

I followed some solid advice from Ramit Sethi, author of *I Will Teach You to Be Rich* and creator of the online course Earn 1K, which I took during my pause. According to Ramit, it's useful to ask at least five others who know you to help you better understand what your strengths are.[12] When I did this, I noticed recurring themes and keywords. I heard "relationship builder, networker, people person." These descriptors formed the bridge that connected my true sense of self to where I shined the most.

I listened to everyone and added their feedback to my pink spiral notebook. I followed my pause plan, which at this point consisted of "Ask others what I am good at." Asking felt empowering, and what I heard back was more empowering. I embraced and accepted what people told me were my natural gifts. I felt affirmed. I was building confidence every time someone shared his or her thoughts. It was like breathing air rich with oxygen and it was a relief. I learned I was good at relating to others and that I was good at creating relationships. I remembered that I knew my industry, the online ad business, inside and out. I possessed many advantages that were in my favor: I was funny, I was smart, and I could do anything. I felt like I had a purpose again. I began to regain my sense of self and remember that my strengths were not just good but magnetic qualities. I could choose a job where my strengths, as McQuaid tells us, would help me flourish.

I didn't realize it then, but I was creating a deeper level of intimacy with myself. I was opening myself up to others and asking for input in ways I hadn't ever done before. I was taking my first steps to cultivate what psychologist and author David Schnarch calls "self-validated intimacy," defined as providing support for myself while letting myself be known.[13] When I shared that I was reassessing my career and figuring out what to do next, I wasn't concerned with what others thought about my actions. When I asked others for their feedback, I risked hearing something negative, or nothing nice at all. For the first time in a long time, perhaps the first in my life, I wasn't looking for approval from others, which is what Schnarch refers to as "other-validated intimacy." Each time I posed the question "What do you consider my strengths?" I created an opportunity to add to my self-validation, take in the positive feedback, and affirm who I was as a result. It felt vulnerable, scary, and liberating.

Who couldn't use a little more self-validated intimacy? How could you do something similar? Start with your SFD, then set your intention and discover your strengths. Let the rest flow from there.

 Ideas for Setting Intention

From the list below, see what works best and give it a try.

1. Focus on something you want to achieve and write down how you intend to achieve it. (Example: *Identify my strengths while I connect with others.*)
2. Pick one word a day to orient toward. It can be the word "intention" or some other word that signals a certain way of being or an attitude you want to take for the day. Do this as a ritual before you get out of bed in the morning.
3. Share your intention with someone in a positive way. Let him or her know what you intend to do about it. (Example: *Tell the person I speak with*

that I am reassessing my career and looking for feedback on what they believe I am naturally good at.)

4. Commit to an action that will help you meet
your intention. (Example: *I will make a list of people I want to talk to and schedule time to ask them
what my strengths are.*)

5. Think about what you could do to feel fulfilled
and add to your own self-validated intimacy.
Write down your intention. Before you go to
bed, reread it.

6. Share with a friend how you felt while creating
your intention. Maybe you'll inspire your friend
to do something similar. You can ask him or her
to partner with you for a week to exchange intentions.

7. Spend five minutes thoughtfully journaling
about how you came to plan a meaningful
pause. Was it picking up this book? Was it allowing yourself a few minutes to be and not do?
Was it sharing your plan with a friend? Did you
surrender and trust in the outcome, knowing all
will unfold in its own due time?

Step 3: Create Your Plan

Even though you want to surrender to a pause and plunge in,
it's important to know *how* you want to spend your time pausing. Your plan does not need to be specific or detailed. It is
better to leave it somewhat vague and open. In my case, I
created a framework for a few things I knew I wanted to do
and left room for the rest to unfold. I wanted to take things

one day at a time. Before you dive into planning, let's explore common ways we like to think we're doing ourselves a favor by planning, when in reality it may not be helpful. This is true especially when we fill our time with nonstop action for the sake of doing things.

Busifying, Doing, and Being

The word *business* has a striking similarity to the word *busyness*. Both share the same root, a fourteenth-century Old English term, *bisignes*. This word means "care, anxiety, occupation" and a "state of being much occupied or engaged."[14] The word *busy* is defined as "full of activity or work" and implies a similar anxious occupation of sorts.[15] To what extent is keeping busy a way to stay occupied? Whether you are at home or at work, doing busywork implies that you have a lot of activities that occupy your time, but they may not necessarily be fulfilling. The question to ask is, Why do we *do* for the sake of *doing*?

When my brother and I were recently planning a trip to visit our mom and stepdad in Syracuse, New York, Drew mentioned he was struck by how so many people, including our well-intentioned mom, Virginia, thrive on keeping busy. He created a verb to describe this behavior: *busify*, which he defined as "to constantly fill time with activities." (I have yet to see it defined anywhere else as this, so as far as I'm concerned, he gets full credit!)

I suspect there are many Virginias among us. Finding the balance between being and doing is different for everyone. It is one of the dualities of the human condition. The *being* in us wants to emerge, present and aware, happy to exist. The *doing* part in us wants to achieve and strive, to accomplish, to be seen, and to make a difference. Both are essential and important pieces of who we are. However, we have lost sight of how important just being is, as we've focused on doing and building in our modern society. With so many of us busifying our lives, it is easy to forget how powerful doing nothing is. Ideally, pausing can become a way of life. Whether we're at work or elsewhere, pausing is a skill. It takes practice and conscious effort, especially for my fellow overachiever, doer types. My mom is no different from many of us, for whom doing is a way of life we have grown to know and love. We do things because they make us feel good. As a result, we feel fulfilled and accomplished. How often do any of us stop to ask ourselves, What activities are contributing to my overall (well-)being?

At work we do the same thing. In our culture, the busier we are at work, the more productivity and profits can follow. Standing around appearing idle conjures up an image of a slacker, or someone who is wasting precious time. What if that time is spent pausing *because of* a problem you're trying to solve? It may look like you are daydreaming, but actually this is one of the most creative and productive states of mind, and data and research from multiple studies prove it.

In a 2013 article in *Scientific American*, author Ferris Jabr summarizes the benefits of daydreaming and shares insights from studies about time spent at work managing information:[16]

> *Some studies have demonstrated that the mind obliquely solves tough problems while daydreaming—an experience many people have had while taking a shower. Epiphanies seem to come out of nowhere, but they are often the product of unconscious mental activity during downtime. A 2010 LexisNexis survey of 1,700 white collar workers in the U.S., China, South Af-*

rica, the UK, and Australia revealed that on average employees spend more than half their workdays receiving and managing information rather than using it to do their jobs, half of the surveyed workers also confessed that they were reaching a breaking point after which they would not be able to accommodate the deluge of data.

What if pausing was woven into corporate culture by making skill-based self-awareness and emotional intelligence training part of a minimum requirement of an employee profile? This is the power of pausing, and the potential it carries personally and professionally. It can become a way of life to balance out our "always doing" lives.

The Key to Planning a Pause: Deep Listening

There are two meanings to what I call "deep listening." The first meaning relates to listening to your inner voice and following your intuition. It is a guide for planning your pause. Whatever questions may arise, it's about tuning inward and paying attention to what you feel cultivates compassion for yourself and others. You can develop your plan as you practice deep listening. It isn't about jumping into the next thing because you suddenly feel uncomfortable with a new routine (or lack of one). Deep listening is when you allow your inner voice to emerge and share what your plan is in the first place. It's all too easy to miss it. It's easy to drown out this voice with the distractions and noise of everyday life.

I believe one of the biggest blocks to deep listening is when we busify ourselves and fill our lives up and miss the cues that deep listening provides. The plan that our intuition is pointing us toward becomes drowned out or goes unheard when all that needed to happen was to allow your inner voice to be heard.

Prior to my pause, deep listening to my inner voice took place, but only to a certain extent. I liked to cut it off or not allow it to have too much airtime. I chose to stay busy to avoid tuning in to myself and feeling at a deeper level. If I had stopped to listen to my inner voice or my true guidance system, I would have heard something along these lines:

Why do you ignore me?
Why are you doing so much?
Why are you working so hard to avoid me?

I was too scared to be alone with my thoughts and feel how unhappy and isolated I was. On some level I knew that if I sat still and listened, I would learn something about myself that I wasn't likely ready to acknowledge. My pause forced me to deeply listen to my own inner voice. I listened to this voice and heard that my plan should focus on not making plans. Everything else would be a distraction. It was time to get real and be fully present with myself.

Deep Listening as a Way of Life

The benefits of deep listening go far beyond planning for a pause. It can help you tune in to how you are feeling and your presence in any given moment. What works for you? Focus on how your body feels and settle into yourself. Allow your mind to quiet. Take in your surrounding sensory-grounded data— what you see, hear, taste, touch, and smell. If you find your thoughts spinning mindlessly, simply bring attention to your breath.

Try deep listening while performing an activity you enjoy. Expect the occasional distraction. The key is to recognize when this happens, catch it, and return back to your deep listening "in the zone" state. Focus on your breath, and use your sensory perception. What do you see, feel, hear, taste, or smell as you move? During your activity, chances are you will feel more engaged, alive, and in tune with yourself as a result.

Deep listening can happen anytime. I happen to find it often in physical exercise. When I get into a boat in the Oakland Bay, I am present in the here and now. Cooking, gardening, or flying a kite can all be ways to find a meditative or deep listening state. When your body is physically engaged, you are more likely to come up with an idea, resolution, or realization. Your inner voice emerges from this space. Imagine your inner voice appearing like a thought bubble over your head in a comic strip. Only you hear it, but it is relevant and important communication you need to know. Ask yourself:

What am I feeling?
What happened recently that caused me to feel a certain way?

We all adopt different ways to heal. Deep listening can lead you to de-busify your life, repair a relationship, or move closer to your vision of who you want to become. There's plenty of research that shows deep listening can slow down resting heart rate, reduce levels of stress, and raise what HeartMath Institute research director Rollin McCraty calls "heart coherence," or the ability to synchronize our physical, mental, and emotional systems. "It is a state that builds resiliency—personal energy is accumulated, not wasted—leaving more energy to manifest intentions and harmonious outcomes," says Dr. McCraty.[17] Like a form of meditation, deep listening allows your thoughts to flow and attune to your own body, mind, and inner voice.

There is nothing wrong with filling your days with activities you love. These are the enjoyments and pleasures of life. They matter. If you are passionate about what you're doing, you become happier and more fulfilled. Deep listening is one way to figure out your motives and whether you're doing what serves you. Are you passionate about something you love in a way that feeds your spirit? If you're on the right track, your entire being—your mind, body, and soul—will answer a resounding yes. Or are you trudging through something because you "have to get it done," even if it is taking a toll on your physical, mental, or emotional health? What can you do to help your own deep listening skills?

Taking the Pause Plunge: Putting It All Together

You've explored different ways of thinking about a pause: first creating a rough draft, then setting intention, and finally practicing deep listening to hear your inner voice. It is time to put it all together.

Imagine your ideal pause for a few minutes. Think big! Put this book down and spend a few moments daydreaming about the pause-abilities. How would you occupy (or not occupy) your time? How would things be different? What do you see, hear, feel? Think about a few specific things you have postponed or want to pursue that are aligned with your inner voice (e.g., learn a new skill, have a new perspective, deepen a relationship with a person or a group, just be). A great way to test these out is to tune in to how your body feels as you picture yourself in each pause scenario. Do you feel relaxed or is your body tight or constricted? These are signs you can pay close attention to as you deeply listen to your inner voice.

Remember to go for satisfying your yearnings. You may have obvious surface-level wishes (e.g., hang out in Bali), but what else can you do to feel fulfilled that can be intentional?

Other questions to ask as you plan your pause:

- Who would support you on this journey?
- What do you hope are your motives to take this pause?
- What are you afraid to write down or admit?
- What would you consider a successful pause? (Be specific.)
- Imagine yourself two years from now. What advice would you give yourself as you plan?

Congratulations! You just created your first iteration of your pause plan.

Practice of Pause Moments:
Chapter 3

Step 1: Write your rough draft of why you want to pause. Use Brené Brown's "SFD" approach and include the story you are making up, your emotions, your body, your thinking, your beliefs, your actions.

Step 2: Set your intention for the next twenty-four hours. Keep it simple. What do you want to create for yourself? Write your intention down on a sticky note and put it where you'll see it. Journal about it and, afterward, how it went.

Step 3: Create and journal on your pause plan. Review the questions above about your pause plan. Journal about your ideal pause. One fun way to do this is to write a letter to yourself from your inner voice. Start off with, "What you plan to do on your pause is . . ." and go from there. What would a successful outcome look and feel like? What would you intend to do or not do? How will you and your life be different as a result of your pause?

Chapter 4

The Art of Mental Flossing

The purpose of childhood is formation.
The purpose of adulthood is transformation.

—JACK MEZIROW

Now THAT YOU have a better understanding of setting intention and creating a pause that meets your yearnings, the next step is to deepen your awareness of what you can create, and make the most out of what works for you. Your pause can be a minute, one day, or several weeks. It can be a paid vacation or an unpaid leave of absence. It can be a hiatus between two jobs or any other change. With the right growth mindset, anything is pause-able!

Why is creating an optimal frame of mind so important? As adults we have choices that weren't options when we were younger. We get to choose our frames of reference, what transformational educator Jack Mezirow called "perspective transformation."[1] As children we undiscerningly adapt and mold to our environment. It reminds me of fish in a fish tank, existing and knowing no more than their immediate surroundings. Fortunately, we've evolved way past fish. As humans, and as adults, we are capable of realizing our limits and choosing to take action or make changes that serve us in the here and now. We have the choice to shift from autopilot thinking to autonomous thinking.

When you consciously become more aware of your surroundings, thoughts, reactions, and emotions, you increase your capacity of awareness in everyday life. This ability to tune in to your thoughts and expand your awareness around them is what I call "mental flossing."

We are ruled by our subconscious behaviors unless we do something about it and improve our human relationships through deeper engagement. From what the research and experts in the field share, it becomes a no-brainer why we need to take inventory of what goes on in our own heads. Consider the following:[2]

- Your unconscious mind is a million times more powerful than your conscious mind.
- Your conscious mind's prefrontal cortex alone processes forty nerve impulses per second, while 90 percent of your unconscious brain processes forty million nerve impulses per second.
- As infants, our brains get "wired" through our interactions with our parents, creating the unconscious pathways that underlie a complexity of unconscious beliefs, feelings, and behavior patterns—our sense of self, beliefs about ourselves, what the world expects from us, and what we can expect from the world.
- During the first seven years of life, we download our programming, our "operating system"—for each of us, this will continue to be the way we run our lives unless we

consciously change our complex of unconscious govern-
ing beliefs.

The more you examine research like the above, the clearer
it becomes that our lives are ruled by the beliefs and habits
that come from our family and upbringing. This is related to
a core concept in psychology called attachment theory. How
we experience attachment with our primary caregivers affects
how we deal with emotions and informs our thoughts, beliefs,
self-esteem, and relationships with others later in life.[3] This is
why our early years (including while we are in the womb!)
play a critical role in how our neural pathways develop as well
as our emotional capacity.

Why Mental Flossing Matters

Fortunately for us, adults are designed to transform, or move
toward who we can become, thanks to neuroplasticity. Neuroplasticity is the brain's potential to adapt or create new neural pathways as we learn and grow. It's what helps us when we
engage in our mental flossing and shift our beliefs. Knowing
you have the ability to build new neural circuitry is a big reason why pausing can help anyone looking to create change.
Our transformation circuits are activated with our intentional
shift in behavior and the choice to do so.[4]

The false beliefs (also known as limiting or mistaken beliefs)
about yourself, the world, and others that you developed as a
child based on limited views and experiences may not be in your
best interest later in life. Having these beliefs is human nature.
Everybody has them. Once accepted, you see how your mental

chatter may or may not be in your best interest. You are taking what was unconscious and shining a light on it. Like anything under a big bright spotlight, it shows up more clearly. This is the idea behind mental flossing. By witnessing your thoughts and catching them in the moment, you are shining a light on them so that you can shift them to serve you best.

Each time you catch a thought that is from an outdated belief system, pause. Even if it's only for a strobe light instant, you can consciously shift your behavior and move from mind-less "monkey mind" mode to a more conscious way of thinking. Pausing creates the space to catch these moments. It is a chance to align with more intentional attitudes and beliefs, which lead to new behaviors and actions.

If your brain is full of chatter, or narratives that don't serve you, that takes its toll. The brain was made to adapt thanks to its neuroplasticity. This includes adapting to environments that are not conducive to happiness and health. The more you have heard your inaccurate narrative, false or limiting beliefs, or anything not in your best interest, the more ingrained it becomes in your neural networks.[5] I'm reminded of the expressions "You are what you think" and "Words shape the world in which we live."

The more you practice mental flossing, the more you change your inner world, through exercising neuroplasticity. Think of it as a workout for your limbic brain. You create new neural pathways and synapses every time you catch a limiting belief, raise awareness around it, and react with a different course of action, behavior, or emotion. The more you practice, the more pathways and networks are created, and the deeper they become over time. When your inner world changes, everything changes, including what you experience in everyday life.

Limiting, Mistaken, or False Beliefs

Mental chatter often takes the form of things you tell yourself that are not in your best interest.

> *I'm not good enough.*
> *I can't stand my* [insert body part of choice here].
> *I am not good at* [insert activity or school subject].

And so it goes.

Mental flossing can shift and shape thoughts so they become more constructive. When you expand your mental awareness and get in the routine of doing so, you can reprogram your thoughts so they are in your best interest. Just like going to the gym, your mind needs mental training to keep your thoughts healthy and helpful.

Mental flossing is an art. It requires skill and practice and a growth mindset. Over time, you can refine your skills and, like an artist, become better at your craft. (Dweck's book mentioned earlier contains a helpful illustration of this in action.) Everyone is capable of learning how to practice mental flossing. The key is figuring out what works for you.

Take Inventory of Your Mental Library

Like any home improvement project, it is important to know what your foundation looks like so you can build and improve upon it. Preparing for what-ifs during a pause may stir up a lot of limiting beliefs. I would be surprised if that didn't happen. Do you hear a lot of mental chatter about obstacles? Or do you have a list of reasons why a pause may not be the right thing to do next? It is easy to panic when we do not have any finite answers and stare uncertainty in the face.

I like to think of all our memories, beliefs, behaviors, and experiences as files, or "recorded tapes," stored in our mental libraries. (The word "tape" is so ingrained in my vocabulary as a child of the eighties. Record, CD, or MP3 may make more sense to you.) Each can be checked out, used, and then put back on the shelf and filed away.

One of the most common defense mechanisms our brains have is to select a "fear tape" out of our mental library. You probably recognize it as it plays. It may be loud, and it may start playing when you least expect it. It may be a limiting belief or a fear that comes up and is warning you to not proceed, or to use extreme caution if you decide to do so. This is where mental flossing comes in handy. Be aware of when this happens, catch it in the moment (or when you realize it has happened), and recognize it as one of the tapes from your mental library. It doesn't mean your fear doesn't exist. But now that you know it exists, you can replace it with an updated, more constructive tape that leads you to take your next action, not prevent it.

The messages on these tapes usually sound like this:

General false fear tape: *There's no way I can pull this off. What if I fail?* On this tape, your brain finds *any* excuse on hand to prevent you from making your next move.

Finances tape: *How can I pay for this? There's no way I can save that much money. I am such a bad saver/big spender. I don't have enough savings. I don't have a steady income.* On this tape, money is the excuse for not taking action.

Loss-of-control tape: *How will I live? What will happen to* *me? What if I don't like* [the activity or plan]*? I won't feel comfortable if I go through with this.* This tape prevents you from taking action because there are too many unknowns and variables beyond your control.

Lack-of-approval tape: *What will my* [friends/family/partner] *think of me making this type of decision?* This tape uses the fear of others' disapproval to keep things status quo.

Self-sabotage tape: *I will fail anyway. Why should I do this now? What good will that do? There's no way I can learn anything new. This is a waste of time.* This tape is designed to talk yourself out of any action by using a list of your insecurities.

These false fear tapes are running all the time. Note that I don't describe them as "negative." They don't have to be bad, and the idea isn't to erase them or ignore them. That only exacerbates the problem. What is important is to accept that they are outdated recordings—the archives of your mental library. They are no longer relevant. The key to updating these tapes is recognizing what beliefs serve your highest good and creating new mental tapes, or new beliefs, that serve you. One tool to help you do this is to TASER your thoughts: tune in, acknowledge, shift, express, repeat.

The Art of TASERing

The next time you notice one of your mistaken beliefs surfacing, use what I call the "TASER technique." Just like with a Taser stun gun, you can "zap" your thoughts in the moment. You can TASER a false belief and stop it in its tracks. As you

⑪ Beware the Amygdala Hijack

It's easy to stir up a lot of discomfort as you observe your thoughts and start sorting through your mental library of mistaken beliefs and fear tapes. Many times, and not surprisingly, we revert back to our old patterns and habitual ways of thinking (neurologically, we return to our brain's familiar and already wired pathways). Our higher-level-thinking brain, the prefrontal cortex, goes offline and our emotional center takes precedence.[6] When this happens, we are more likely to experience tunnel vision and get caught up in our limbic system's emotional response. It dominates all or most of our attention, and doing anything else well becomes nearly impossible. What's going on underneath the surface is that the almond-shaped cluster of neurons known as the amygdala lights up from all the emotional stimulation, and it can prompt instantaneous survival responses. Most, if not all, of us have experienced what it's like when this occurs. This is an amygdala hijack. We literally feel hijacked from our rational, conscious way of thinking.

practice TASERing over time, your awareness of thoughts or beliefs that do not serve you will increase.

This is a great tool when you are planning your pause, but it doesn't need to be limited to only then. It can be used in any area of your life. You've spent years—your entire lifetime—listening to these false belief tapes. It's time to TASER them:

Tune in. When you hear one of your limiting beliefs, tune in. Catching it in the moment is ideal, but even after the fact is helpful.

Acknowledge what you've heard and that these are familiar recordings your mind plays. Your brain is practicing what it knows and expects. It's okay that this recording is there. It is playing a tape based on your experiences, past history, environment, life, and/or limited views you once had as a child. In the spirit of a kind and gentle caregiver watching over yourself, acknowledge what you've heard. Avoid beating yourself up about it.

Shift this false belief to a new belief. This is a more accurate, conscious representation of yourself. As an example, if your false belief is "I *am not* good enough," shift your new belief to the exact opposite. In this case, "I *am* good enough." Your updated, new belief becomes something that serves you and you can orient toward.

Express your new belief. Think of your kind, loving voice again. Say your new belief out loud, such as, "I am enough" (the opposite of your historical false belief). Express out loud any feelings, such as, "I feel fear right now" or "I feel joy." By stating your new belief and feelings out loud, your brain neurologically starts to think differently as you engage your prefrontal cortex and signal it to think more intellectually about your state, versus actually experiencing that state.[7] The act itself helps bring your higher-thinking brain back online. Refrain from judgment. Don't be overly critical. Simply experience the moment.

Repeat the process every time you catch a false, outdated belief surfacing. Repeating the process is critical to construct new neural pathways and encode them. This has positive, long-term effects. You likely have heard the statistic that it takes ten thousand hours to develop mastery in anything, whether you are an Olympic athlete, a meditative monk, or a musical genius.[8] Shifting how you think is no different, and given that we are awake and conscious for two thirds of our existence, how you spend your waking hours counts. As you practice TASERing moment by moment, this final step keeps you dedicated, which is critical to long-term creation and shaping of new beliefs. As with any skill, with practice you will undoubtedly become more proficient as you shift your beliefs.

Like grooves on a pressed record, these are new grooves in your neural pathways. As a result, new feelings and thoughts are likely to emerge. On a physiological and neurological level, your brain is literally changing how you think, behave, and feel. Every new belief creates a new neural pathway in your brain. Repeating these new beliefs shifts your habits and ways of thinking. Use the TASERing technique for at least one false belief a day and aim to use it any time you catch a false belief. The more often you consciously tune in to your mental library, you become more aware of your thoughts by default. You are clearing out the historical beliefs that no longer serve you.

Add the word "historically" to any statement about a limiting belief. "I don't ask for what I want" becomes "Historically, I don't ask for what I want." This helps shift to a more accurate, present-time belief.

"Inviting Mara to Tea" Meditation Practice

Meditation is more than just blissing out. It can be used to tune in on an emotional level and feel more in your body. Psychologist and Buddhist meditation teacher Tara Brach discusses full acceptance of all our emotions in her book *Radical Acceptance*. One practice she uses, called "Inviting Mara to Tea," uses the same principles as the "name it to tame it" technique.[9] The idea is that if you are meditating, you can recognize your emotions, instead of suppressing them, by stating how you feel over and over again as a mantra. For example, if you feel anger, say out loud, "Anger, anger, anger." This has a similar affect as the previous exercise: you acknowledge what you are feeling, engage your prefrontal cortex, and allow the emotion to complete and flow through you.

PAUSE STORY
Mike Robbins

*From Stressed-Out Professional Baseball Player
to Authenticity Expert*

Entrepreneur Mike Robbins exemplifies the positive effects of mental flossing and TASERing thoughts. Fresh out of Stanford and a Division I baseball team, Mike began his career as a pitcher for the Kansas City Royals in the minor leagues. It wasn't long before an injury cut his pitching career short and forced him to look into other options for work.

Budget: Whatever savings he had at the time

Duration: Five months

Goal: Find his calling

Trigger: Wondering what to do after his career-altering injury, Mike took a job in sales for the Internet advertising company 24/7 Media and, later, Rivals.com, which, in the dot-com boom of the 1990s, was on pace to go public. Like many others in mid-2000, Mike received notice that the company was downsizing in the slowing market and economy. Stressed out and freaked out, Mike wondered what to do next.

Plan: Mike wanted to start looking for work immediately. It seemed like the next logical step. As he set out on his job search, he started thinking about other big life-changing decisions he wanted to make. He broke up with his girlfriend. He chose to stay in San Francisco instead of moving to Los Angeles, a decision he had been contemplating for months.

Mike decided to stop his job search. He packed his bags and made a plan to backpack for a few months, something he had on his bucket list of things to do before it was too late. For the following five months, Mike fulfilled one of his biggest dreams. He stopped in Sydney and became inspired watching the 2000 Olympic games. After the games, Mike ventured to London, Paris, and New York, all places he'd long wanted to visit.

The world appeared new again. This new perspective reminded Mike how much he longed for more in his life. He yearned to live and work somewhere he could grow and flourish. As exciting as his short stint working in the Internet industry had been, he thought about how he could live more fully and feel, every day, the same way he felt while on his adventure.

Impact: Mike returned to San Francisco in late 2000 and met his future wife, Michelle, in a personal development course at Landmark Education (now Landmark Worldwide). While he was focused on his own growth and becoming more aware of what he could do differently, and how he could incorporate it all into his world, he felt inspired. He felt called to help others. He wanted more for himself. He also set his sights on writing his first book.

Today, fifteen years into his coaching and consulting business, Mike speaks to Fortune 500 companies and private clients, sharing his message of gratitude and how to express it daily. His core theory is that if you express and feel gratitude, authentically and in the moment, you are more fulfilled and more successful in all areas of your life. His message is an important one: whether it's business or personal, physical or mental, gratitude and appreciation make a difference in how you feel and how others interact with you. It is a valuable message and one that more people need to hear.

Postpause, Mike has written three books, *Be Yourself, Everyone Else Is Already Taken; Focus on the Good Stuff;* and *Nothing Changes Until You Do.* He's spoken at numerous conferences, including three TED conferences about gratitude and authenticity, two of his favorite subjects. He and Michelle have two daughters, and Mike makes sure to express his gratitude to his family, his clients, and his friends. If you call Mike and you get his voice mail, he encourages you to tell him one thing that you are grateful for that day. Now, that's a powerful (voice) message.

PRACTICE OF PAUSE ADVICE

Jump and find your wings on the way down.
If you take the leap, trust that you will land on your own
two feet in a new and inviting place.

You are ready even if you don't think you are.
Your brain is a skilled expert in diversionary tactics and
can get you to think and believe almost anything. Instead,
believe in yourself and that you are ready for a change, a
pause, or taking on something new. You can always plan,
do, and prepare more, but unless you attempt to do something (instead of just planning for it), it's easy to get stuck
in an endless cycle of planning.

Ask for and be willing to receive support.
It's okay to ask for help. Share your plan with others who
will support and help you along the way. Everything becomes easier when you have others who can help you when
you need it. Let them know that you need them and how
they can help you. Chances are highly likely that they will!

Act "As If"

William James (1842–1910), a leading philosopher and
psychologist of his time, believed happiness is created as
a result of being an active participant in the game of
life.[10] James thought that if people acted "as if" they
possessed a specific quality, belief, or attitude, that en-

abled them to embody and create those behaviors. James wrote, "Be not afraid of life. Believe that life *is* worth living, and your belief will help create the fact."[11] This concept goes by another name: "Fake it 'til you make it." Act as if you matter (or create the new belief that you matter), and you are more likely to feel that way.

Practice of Pause Moments:
Chapter 4

Inventory of Your Historical Limiting Beliefs

Fold or draw a line on a piece of paper lengthwise so you have two columns. Write down your limiting beliefs related to your pause on the left side. Here are a few examples: *I will run out of money if I take an extended pause. I don't deserve to slow down. I am too busy to pause or figure out what would work for me.* Avoid absolute words like "always," "never," "must," etc.

Circle the limiting belief or beliefs that resonate with you the most (e.g., any that make you think, "I have that one, *big-time*").

Next to each belief, write down a new belief to replace it in the right-hand column.

Review your updated list of new beliefs in the right-hand column. How can you start acting "as if" and embracing your updated beliefs?

Chapter 5

The Pause Dashboard: Money, Time, and Activity

Unless commitment is made,
there are only promises and hopes; but no plans.

—PETER DRUCKER

NOW THAT YOU KNOW how mental flossing can help you create an ideal mindset for your pause, it's important to understand how you can structure your pause to meet your resources. No matter what you decide to do, you have three dials to gauge what is right for you.

The Three Pause Dials

- Money
- Time frame
- Activity

There's no secret formula for creating a pause. It is an art. Depending on your flexibility and how creative you get, you can adjust these dials on your pause dashboard.

Unfortunately, many people don't consider pausing. They

mistakenly think it costs too much or they don't have enough time. Just because you don't have a stash of savings doesn't mean you have to take a shorter pause, and just because you have a rich bank account doesn't mean you can pause forever. It all depends on what you do and how you do it.

The truth is that anyone can take a pause; it's people's fear of the unknown and their limiting beliefs that stop them. For example, you already paused and picked up this book. Since you invested time to read, you are gifting yourself time and space to learn how it can work for you. Pausing is creating a shift in behavior so that you are more present with yourself. Everything else is secondary.

The Money Dial

Who doesn't want more money? Let's face it, finances are usually the freakiest part of planning anything. Figuring out what is within or beyond your means matters. Regardless of your type of pause, creating a budget and assessing it can help you plan. With a little creative planning, your finances don't need to severely limit what you do.

A few questions to consider:

If you take paid leave, why not take the maximum time offered?

If you take unpaid leave, what can you comfortably afford to do with that time?

For instance, your pause can be essentially free. Maybe you want to take a class but need more savings. What could you sell or trade for more cash? What could you do to save a little more or create a new revenue stream? Maybe your pause will be a day hike, or maybe you'll spend your life savings on a luxury retreat (although I don't recommend this option). You get the point. Find the budget you are willing to spend, and the pause plan will follow.

For those who need to budget for a longer time off, this section is for you. I've broken it down to simple terms: first establish a budget based on the expenses you think you would have during your pause. Then create your savings plan based on what you require for the time off.

Use the Don't Break the Bank worksheet on my Web site (also noted in the "Further Resources" section of this book) for an in-depth review of budgeting. You'll assess your monthly expenses for fixed costs (rent or mortgage payments, utilities, etc.) and variable costs (discretionary income) and compare it to your after-tax income.[1] Once you have an estimate for what you can save, your options become more flexible.

Thinking big and getting creative helps. When you are unable to increase your savings, there's no reason to panic. You can adjust your pause time frame and/or activities. Do what's realistic. If you know you have six weeks before you pause and can save one hundred dollars per week, you can adjust your activities to accommodate a six-hundred-dollar budget.

PAUSE STORY
Alfie van der Zwan

*From Burned-Out Management Consultant
to Engaged Citizen*

Sometimes savings can stretch far beyond what is originally thought possible. Like me, Alfie van der Zwan felt called to slow down and maximize his time off. He got creative and stretched his budget for two years as he traveled all over the world resourcefully.

Budget: Approximately $15,000 for one year

Duration: The plan was three months, which turned into two years

Goal: See the world and search for deeper meaning in his life

Trigger: Alfie held a well-paid management consulting job, which left him unfulfilled and feeling like he was no longer learning or growing. He found himself in a city and in a relationship that weren't making him happy. Alfie felt helpless and unsure that he could control or change anything. His life felt heavy, drained, and tiring. He was stuck. After having reached what he knew was his breaking point, he knew something had to change—and realized that something was him. He decided to take a two-and-a-half-month pause—a break of unpaid leave. As he was a star employee, his employer was happy to oblige, knowing he would return.

Plan: Alfie left his consulting life and began his trip around the world. He decided to start in the Middle East—Jordan—because it interested him and because he knew being there would break familiar patterns. His intention was to do as little as possible that resembled his previous routine, so he left behind everything that resembled what he called his "stuck" life. During this time, he started to regain his confidence, and at the end of the two and a half months he returned to work.

However, after three months back on the job, Alfie realized he still had a lot to learn about himself and life. He wanted to return to the road and continue to explore who and what he was and wanted to be. He gave notice, bought a one-way ticket to Asia, and devised a loose plan.

Alfie was fortunate to have saved enough cash to travel freely. His goal was to stretch his funds for as long as possible. He left his home base of Johannesburg with savings in hand. Traveling around Asia and Southeast Asia, Alfie stayed in budget hotels, some costing just five and ten dollars per night. It was far from luxury, but it was all he needed. Alfie's adventurous eating habits came in handy. He ate street food with the locals, which often meant he was able to eat three-course meals for two or three dollars and still have money for a five-dollar massage! He chose local transport over the pricier tourist options and would group together with other travelers to negotiate group discounts. Every dollar saved bought him more traveling time.

Alfie had friends he wanted to visit, and he drifted between cities and countries. He tried new things at every opportunity. He met different people and let go of controlling every aspect of his life. It was time to do the opposite and see what there was to gain. After all, controlling everything before hadn't worked out so well. It was definitely time to be in the flow of letting life guide him.

Impact: By immersing himself in a completely different environment, Alfie became more aware of his behaviors, patterns, reactions, and beliefs. He has integrated his pause mentality back into his daily life. He can still tap into how he felt on his pause and he no longer feels stuck.

Today, Alfie is much happier. He has a newfound joy for life. He met his wife, Ariane, on his pause. They currently live in Cape Town, South Africa, and are the proud parents of a young son. They also created a mobile app called Mindful365. After his pause, Alfie started working at a social enterprise company that aligns with his yearning to have an impact on people's lives. Alfie continues to assess his career and make corresponding changes. He knows it's a journey for finding his next adventure or challenge, whatever it may be. As a result of his pause, Alfie strives to act quickly rather than taking years to reach a breaking point, as he once did. Most importantly, Alfie feels confident to make any change. He trusts his decisions and believes that life will take care of him and that he can choose to create the life he desires.

PRACTICE OF PAUSE ADVICE

Get uncomfortable.
Get out of your comfort zone. Wear clothes that are different from your normal look. Get a new haircut. Take a different route to work. Move to a different city or country. Do anything! Be sure it scares you a little (or a lot). You'll get a little braver every time.

Change your environment.
Extract yourself from your existing environment. You

will be forced to learn and create new patterns, behaviors, and actions. Take a class for something you've never done before, travel somewhere you've never been (even if it's only for a weekend), or join a new group that shares one of your passions. Join a local community around a particular subject or hobby, and, as Meetup.com says, "find your people."

Take small steps.
If you can't make a big change, start with one small change. As you begin to make small steps, making more changes will become more and more comfortable. A bunch of little steps add up over time and can lead to big changes that wouldn't have happened otherwise.

The Time Dial

How much time are you willing or able to pause? Depending on your work situation, flexibility, and vacation schedule, you may already know the answer to that. Pausing can also be scheduled around destinations you already plan to visit.

Pausing Without Quitting Your Job

This is a great way to take your pause with minimal risk. Do you have two, three, or four weeks of vacation accrued? Think about how you can pause without leaving your day job. Don't let timing limit your ideas. It is possible to keep a paycheck and have a meaningful pause.

Paid pauses of all lengths are always a good idea. Here are a few examples that vary in length. Each one had a powerful and positive impact, with minimum financial impact or effort to plan.

One or a Few Days: Take a Daylong Time-Out

My friend Holly is a single mom with a six-year-old daughter. She takes daylong time-outs about once a month. She recently spent an entire weekday at a monastery a few hours from home. She had never visited a monastery before, let alone spent an entire day at one. She liked the idea of being in a secluded, serene environment where everyone was focused on inner thoughts and awareness. She was in good company and enjoyed silent walks outside, communal meals, and participating in silent group meditation. She didn't leave her job to do it, and this one day made a huge difference to her peace of mind and work-life balance.

One Week: Be a Tourist in Your Own City or Town

When I lived in New York City, my rowing friend Greg announced he was taking a week vacation . . . in New York City. He planned to be a tourist and do all the cool things he didn't normally do as a resident. I thought he was crazy, but the more I thought about it, the more I saw how brilliant it was. He had found a way to unwind without leaving his home.

In one week, Greg visited the Metropolitan Museum of Art, the Statue of Liberty, Central Park, and neighborhoods he didn't usually frequent. He rowed every morning, and he would share with us what his tourist attraction was for that day. He rejuvenated without breaking the bank. Travel and accommodation costs didn't apply. It was the first time I ever heard of someone intentionally not going anywhere (this was before the term "staycation" was popular). He intentionally stayed home and discovered his backyard. *He paused.* In Greg's case, he focused inward and didn't overplan or overdo. He chose to staycate, not vacate.

All of us are capable of doing something similar. Every town, village, and city has its own undiscovered gems. Put on your tourist hat and see what a pause has to offer you where you live.

The Activity Dial

The art of intention is useful when it comes to activity. Depending on what your intention is and where you are in life, your time off could vary from having a refreshing and renewing staycation to an epic travel experience to a volunteer opportunity in faraway lands. Maybe you need to care for an elder or a baby. Perhaps you need time to research a new job, career, or role.

What images come up when you think about your deepest desires? Can you fulfill your yearnings in a few meaningful activities? If you identify what your yearnings are, you can likely come up with some great activities, given your budget and time frame, that will lead to a rewarding pause.

Here are some examples depending on if you go low budget or high budget, and if you have a little time (a day) or an abundance of time (weeks, months, and beyond!). Think of it like a two-by-two grid:

Lots of time and cheap to moderate: free online classes

such as Khan Academy, YouTube how-to videos, hiking, library visits, training for a sporting event, learning a creative skill such as playing an instrument, dancing, or painting.

Lots of time and expensive: extended world or regional travel, luxury travel, safari, a new hobby or sport that happens to be expensive, like skiing or flight lessons.

Little time and cheap to moderate: park or neighborhood walks, local museum visits, one-time local classes, meet-up groups in an area of interest, fitness classes, meditation at a local community center or home, following your breath, silent meditation retreats, dinner with friends, deepening a relationship, theme parks, picnics, journaling, community yoga, twenty-minute TED Talks or Talks at Google on YouTube. Check out more ideas in chapter 6, "The Daily Pause."

Little time and expensive: one-week trips, an overnight trip to a nearby city or town, a luxury resort overnight stay, a spa visit, weekend or short trip to visit family or friends.

There's no limit to the type of activity you can plan. These are only a few examples. Your creativity, deep-listening skills, and yearnings can guide you in generating ideas. Once that happens, take action to fulfill them meaningfully!

What if your chosen activity centers on making a career shift? Jenny Blake, another Googler, like me, decided to change careers and start her own company after writing a postgraduation advice book, *Life After College*, and blog of the same name.

PAUSE STORY
Jenny Blake

*From Corporate Development and Training
to Entrepreneur and Author*

Having spent five-plus years at Google, Jenny felt she had more to pursue professionally—her own business. While working full-time as an AdWords trainer, then career development program manager, on nights and weekends Jenny developed her passion project, which later became her first book.

Budget: $20,000

Duration: Six months

Goal: Pivot from corporate training and career development and launch her new career as an author, career strategist, and speaker

Trigger: Jenny hit a wall with juggling the project and her full-time role at Google, so she hit pause on the book. In 2010 she vowed "not to let her dream die on the vine" and decided to find an agent so that she could seek a book contract with a traditional publisher. After twenty-seven rejections, she got a yes, and her book was scheduled for release in March 2011.

Plan: Jenny asked for a three-month unpaid leave and organized a self-funded ten-city book tour to coincide with the launch. For three months, Jenny traveled across the country promoting her own book. It was also an opportunity to refresh and renew after working for five-plus years. It was a time to decide whether Google was still the best option at this point. Should she return, or was it better to continue on this new path? As a fellow Googler, I can attest that an unpaid leave at Google is not only one of the best perks there is, but it is tremendously appreciated by its employees.

Impact: Jenny finally figured out what would be best for her life and career and decided to take the plunge into self-employment. Today, Jenny feels happier, healthier, and more fulfilled—fully in charge of her day, her work, her travel schedule and time. Now that Jenny is following her purpose "to be as helpful as possible to as many people as possible," her business supplies the energy she needs to thrive. Jenny "feels very grateful for the opportunity to run her own business at this stage of life." Jenny recently published a book—which I call a cousin to *Pause*—called *Pivot: The Only Move That Matters Is Your Next One.*

PRACTICE OF PAUSE ADVICE

Take time to unwind.
The change process can't be rushed. Allow yourself a few weeks (if not longer) to decompress, without any expectations of what you'll get done or accomplish.

Focus on your health and invigorating morning routines.
One of the best parts of a pause is the ability to make health and fitness a top priority. Focus on getting outside, exercising, meditating, and sleeping and eating well.

Do something fun!
Try not to take time off too seriously. Use it as an opportunity to freely explore, travel, create, and reconnect with people.

Tying It All Together

Use the tools in the reference section to plan out your money, time, and activity plan. Review your ideas. Allow them to marinate. Remember your yearnings and plan to meet what your deeper hungers are. As your ideas sink in, revisit your plan and tweak any dials if they change.

Practice of Pause Moments:
Chapter 5

What are your best- and worst-case scenarios for a pause?

Which dial would be easiest for you to change with a little more creativity or planning: money, time, or activity?

Which dial needs to change for your best-case or ideal pause?

How can you prepare for unexpected changes to savings, time frame, or activity?

What activities do you ideally want to pursue during your pause? Think about your yearnings. If you are constrained by budget or time, what could you do that may not be as expensive or require as much time but still satisfy your deepest hungers?

Chapter 6

The Daily Pause

When things begin accelerating wildly out of control,
sometimes patience is the only answer. Press pause.

—DOUGLAS RUSHKOFF

PAUSING IS A CHANCE to notice your feelings and observe
your surroundings in the here and now. By creating a daily
pause, you allow yourself to be, and *not* think. With this new
space, you can develop presence through sensory perception,
notice bodily sensations, or objectively observe your thoughts
and feelings in the moment. Here are some ways you can
pause daily, and incorporate what I call "a new kind of mindfulness." Experiment with what works best, or try something
new every day to keep things fresh and different.

A New Kind of Mindfulness

Mindfulness isn't only about raising awareness in the present
moment. You can do this through various meditation practices that serve as types of attention training or through other

mindful practices. This new kind of mindfulness is the convergence of your emotional self with an awareness in the moment while orienting toward aliveness. It incorporates bringing your full self to bear.[1] To understand what I mean, pause for a moment and focus your attention on your next breath. Next, ask yourself which primary emotion is closest to what you are feeling in the moment. Is it joy? Sadness? Fear? Anger? Hurt? Allow yourself to be curious about what you are experiencing. Can you continue to focus inward and feel it even more, regardless of how comfortable or uncomfortable you may feel? It may take time to tune in; it may even take multiple tries. I invite you to keep asking yourself how you feel and practicing. Maybe you don't notice any emotion at first, but later, after a few seconds or even a minute or two, you do feel something. Like going to the gym, continuing to tune in is good attention training not only for your conscious mind but also for your emotions. Maybe you notice a judgment come up. When this happens see if you can catch it and apply the TA-SERing technique. You can also say, "That's interesting," and file it away as data. All of this is part of the human experience. The reality is that as humans we are designed to feel and express to the best of our ability.

This new kind of mindfulness accepts all emotions fully, which translates to accepting all parts of ourselves. Emotions are data for us to better understand ourselves.[2] One of the fundamental principles of why we exist as humans is to feel alive through all our feelings and experiences. I encourage you to engage in noticing and acknowledging your emotions as you feel and get more into your body.

As human beings we experience fear that we may be unaware of at any given time. Real fears, related to something life threatening, certainly exist, but most of our fears are false fears, like the outdated belief tapes in your mental library that keep you from taking that next step in your personal or professional life. It may come in the form of a nonchalant thought such as, "How much money should I save this week?" or "Will I have enough time for [insert activity/deadline/work project/relationship]?" It may also show up as a thought that we know we don't have an answer for.

This type of fear, about things beyond our control, is commonly known as existential anxiety. What will happen when I die? Will I get married? What if I run out of money? What if I get cancer? The list goes on. No matter what thought conjures up fear, we have the choice to address it. We can also deny, numb, or tune out an unpleasant or uncomfortable emotion—it's way easier and what many of us, including myself, have learned to do. When we choose to embrace our fears, though it may feel uncomfortable and scary, we can move forward in our lives, take risks, and eventually feel more pleasure in the moment as we become more at one with ourselves—our fears and all.

When you tune in and are aware of what you feel, whether you experience fear, joy, or any other emotion, this is what I consider real mindfulness. Your legs may shake. Your breath may become shallower. This is what it means to be alive! Isn't that the thrill of living? When this happens you are more present to yourself and to everyone else. You create a ripple effect as others you interact with have an opportunity to sense your presence, which helps them be more aware and present, and so on and so forth. This is the new kind of mindfulness that allows you to fully feel and ideally express your emotions as you relate to yourself and to others. As you increase your skills in mindfulness and emotional intelligence, you become one more way our world is a better place.

You can learn to do this on a daily basis, several times throughout the day. As you become more aware of what you feel at all times, this is where the adventure begins. Imagine each moment becoming an invitation to feel more alive in that instant as you notice your emotions and your thoughts. Pausing to intentionally shift your emotion or behavior can happen not only daily, but throughout your day. Learning how to communicate and express comes next, but this is the first step. As Viktor Frankl reminds us, pausing helps you notice what is between the stimulus and the response.[3] I take this to mean that when you pause to notice how you feel or the details in one moment, you have the power to consciously choose an action other than what your unconscious mind would choose.

This is the power of greater self-awareness and conscious emoting: being mindful of how you feel and bringing it into your daily practice of mindfulness. Suddenly each day contains infinite moments for a choice to pause. Every day is different as you listen to the world around you and within you. Some days feel more melodic and full of flow, while other days are a cacophony of emotions coming together. Regardless, when you are mindful of your thoughts and emotions, you move closer to feeling more in tune with yourself, and that is what matters.

Meditation as a Pause

Any pause, regardless of its length or whatever you may feel, is a chance to listen to your inner voice, as we have already discussed. It therefore makes sense that some may think of pausing as synonymous with meditation. That certainly is one scenario and the terms overlap. I think of meditation, which can be a type of attention training, such as following one's breath, as an act of focusing awareness on the present moment and accepting one's feelings, thoughts, or physical sensations in the body. Meditation is a good opportunity to notice everything happening in or outside the body and certainly can be one way to pause.

If you are saying to yourself, "Why would I meditate? I can't sit still for two seconds," or "I don't need to meditate," I ask you, like author and spiritual activist Gabrielle Bernstein asks her audience, "Do you have time to feel like crap?"[4] The message is clear. Everyone has at least one minute. Give yourself that gift.

When I attended Burning Man during my 2011 pause, I met Mark Thornton, who became a dear friend. He had written a book called *Meditation in a New York Minute*, and I read it shortly after meeting him. As his title promised, I found the meditations could be done while doing something else. In other words, I could make any activity I already was doing *mindful* by bringing more self-awareness to it. Each example helped me tune in to my sensations and feelings. It was a great introduction to tuning in to my body and noticing what was happening on the inside as well as in the external world. This is how I started my meditation practice, and I continue to incorporate these practices into my everyday life.

I also aim to meditate before I get out of bed. I wake up, lie still, and recite the following mini meditation, known as the daily prayer in the book *A Course in Miracles* (published by the Foundation for Inner Peace), which I first learned from Gabrielle Bernstein. I modified it to my own version, below.

I clasp my hands together in a prayer position and take three deep, controlled, slow belly breaths. Then I recite, out loud:

Today is [today's date, year].

Dear Spirit (substitute God/Universe/Deity of choice)

Today I ask to be an extension of you.

Today I ask you,

Where would you want me to go?

Who would you want me to meet?

What would you want me to say?

How would you want me to feel?

How would you want me to be?

I invite you to come, sit in my heart, and show me what you got.

Thank you, thank you, thank you.

I breathe a few deeper belly breaths. Next, I meditate with a visualization exercise for a few minutes. I visualize myself walking up a stairway. I'm wearing all white and have a beautiful flowing gown draped over me, which feels great on my skin. I climb slowly, one step at a time, stopping between each one. I inhale and exhale on each step I take. A door awaits me at the top. When I get there, I open the door and am greeted by a warm golden light. Sometimes I hear a voice talk to me, and sometimes the light surrounds and embraces me. I try not to think, only listen.

You can also listen to a recorded meditation or visualization. Depending on your mood, you can experience a walking meditation on your way to work, or while you get ready for your day. Make it a point to notice what you see, hear, taste, smell, and feel emotionally. You can even dance for a few minutes in the morning to move your body and feel more present. I'm no purist, but all of these are ways to be more self-aware and conscious. They are all legit in my book.

In-the-Moment Gut Check

You know you're in the moment if you find yourself registering awareness of your senses—you notice how blue the sky is as you look up, you feel the wind on your face, you identify the smell of pine as you pass a tree, or you focus on a friend's words as they speak. This is pausing. You are observing, not thinking. When you find yourself using any one or more of your senses—seeing, hearing, smelling, tasting, or feeling—without judgment or distracting thoughts, you are present.

Expect Distractions

Being distracted or losing your focus is normal and expected. The key is recognizing that it will happen and not getting discouraged. Instead, recognize it, accept it (you can say, "I'm really distracted right now"), and refocus your energy on your pause.

One-Minute Pauses

It's simple to build in a pause with only one minute of your day.

Belly Breath Pause

One of the easiest ways to pause is by focusing on your breath. Uncross your feet and place both feet firmly on the ground, sitting up straight in a chair without support. Place one hand on your diaphragm, or belly. Slowly inhale through your nose. Allow your diaphragm to push against your hand. Feel the air enter your lungs from the bottom up. Hold your breath a second or two, and then slowly exhale through your mouth. Allow your diaphragm to contract and your hand to follow it as you experience the same sensations in reverse. Keeping your hand on your diaphragm will help you stay aware of your body, but you can count as you inhale, and again as you exhale. If you lose count, start over again, and repeat until you get to ten. Start over when you get to ten.

This pause exercise builds in time to relax, refresh, and renew. Even if it's only sixty seconds, this can alter your mood, thoughts, and feelings for the remainder of your day. When I do this, I feel myself becoming more expansive and open-minded. I feel calmer, more grounded and aware.

> Do your daily pause at a pace that works for you. Try doing it at different times of the day, such as when you first wake up or right before you go to bed. Set a timer so you don't worry about the time. Experiment with keeping your eyes closed one day during your exercise, and then keeping them open the next day. You can experiment with lying down instead of sitting down.

MicroMindfulness™ Stress Buster Pauses

David King Keller, PhD, a business development consultant who lectures on the neuroscience of communication, wrote an entire dissertation on pausing (my hero!). His research is filled with neuroscience-backed data on how the brain changes as a result of introducing what he calls "micro-pausing," and he even trademarked a new name for it: "MicroMindfulness™." The benefits are profound, with research showing stress reduction, increased productivity and heightened alertness when these techniques are practiced a few times during the day.[5] Don't have thirty seconds? Dr. Keller describes three ten-second micro-pausing stress reducers anyone can start using.

1. **Six Deep Breaths.** According to a study of twenty-one thousand people, one of the quickest ways to reduce stress is to take six deep breaths. This will lower heart rate and can move your autonomic nervous condition from the fight-or-flight sympathetic nervous system mode to the more productive higher-functioning parasympathetic nervous system mode. Physiologically, your body is receiving signals to relax based on a slower and more controlled pace of breath. Your shoulders relax, your jaw softens, or your brow unfurrows. Notice how your body feels different as you breathe consciously.

2. **Palm to Face.** Place the palm of one hand close to your face in front of your mouth and blow into the palm, putting all of your attention on the breath and the sensation on your palm. It's very focusing and calming.

3. **Two Palms Together.** Hold the palm of each hand on either side of your face at eye level and try to look at both palms at once. The challenge is enough to distract the amygdala part of the "lower primal" brain that is stressed and place you into a calmer mode run by the higher-functioning, executive-decision-making part of the prefrontal cortex areas of the brain.

David highlights more about MicroMindfulness™ in his forthcoming book, *Are You Worth Thirty Seconds?* (To which we all can reply with an enthusiastic "Hell yes!")

The Five Senses Pause

If I am unable to meditate any morning due to time constraints, I practice this pause. It can be done at any time, including when walking down the street, showering, or brushing your teeth.

No matter what activity you are performing, describe what's happening using your five senses. Tune in to the moment and notice what is going on outside and within you.

What do you see?
What do you hear?
What do you smell?
How do your feet feel in contact with the ground? Or your
    seat on the chair?
What emotion are you feeling?
Where do you feel that in your body?

Close your eyes if possible, continuing your conscious breath. Hear the sounds around you, or the sensations of hot or cold on your face. Or listen to your heart beating.

The Nature Pause

Go outside. If you are unable to get outside, find a color photo or inspiring image. Whether you're outside or looking at a beautiful scene, divide your surroundings up into sections to describe and focus on each. If you're outside, start by looking at the ground and ask, "What is the color of the ground? What's the texture like?" If you see a living tree, a plant, even a blade of grass, ask yourself the same question about that object. Take a deep breath—what does it smell like? Touch or pick up a fistful of dirt and smell the earth, or put your nose next to a flower or tree. What comes to mind as you take in this scent? How do you feel as you describe your surroundings?

As you practice the exercises in this chapter, incorporate one or more of the following self-checks:

- **Tune inward and notice your thoughts and emotions.** If you aren't sure what emotion you're feeling, pick from among the five primary ones whichever one seems closest (fear, hurt, joy, anger, sadness). How many times can you tune in on any one day? Try setting an hourly timer or tune in before a meal. Over time this can become a helpful habit. The more you practice, the easier it will become to feel an emotion at any given time.
- **Body scan:** Imagine a beam of light perpendicular to your body that scans you from head to toe. As the light moves through and down your body, notice how your body feels. Imagine the light dissolving any tension you feel as you breathe into that particular area. Continue until the scan passes through your body. Experiment with starting at the opposite end of your body and as you stand, sit, or lie down.
- **Choose an object that can act as an "anchor," or the focus of your attention.** An anchor can be your breath, a lit candle, or an object in the distance. It is anything that your mind can return to if attention wanders away. Your eyes can be open or closed. Our minds like to wander, so expect that to happen and simply return to your anchor when you notice it.

- Use sensory-based questions to increase your presence. Ask yourself, "What am I noticing? What am I *not* noticing? What do I see? What textures are there? What am I feeling? What do I smell? What sounds are here?"

More Mini Pauses

- A walk outdoors, even if it's just around the block. Similar to the nature walk, stay focused on your sensory experience, emotions, and observations. Invite a friend for this "mindful" walk and explain its purpose. Afterward, discuss with each other what you experienced.
- Sip a cup of tea or coffee without distractions such as checking your phone or talking with anyone else.
- Practice a yoga pose, or have a one-song dance party (or longer) where you move your body by yourself or with others.
- Express gratitude for at least one thing today. You can build your list up to ten things, or set a timer and for one minute express gratitude for everything that comes to mind during that time frame.
- Create a daily one-minute "mindful" awareness pause while you do something else.
- When your head hits the pillow, think of your favorite moment of your day. I give full credit for this practice, which I learned in 2002, to my Intro to Management professor at Fordham. Fifteen years later, I still aim to do this every night before I go to bed. I sleep better, and it is a beautiful moment I can envision. Now you can practice it, too.

PAUSE STORY
Austin Hill Shaw

From Aspiring Architect to Creativity Cultivator
and Founder of Creativity Matters

Austin graduated at the top of his class from architecture school in 2001, and he obtained an academic scholarship to study for one year in Spain's Basque Country. It sounded ideal: he could continue to hone his architecture expertise and brush up on his conversational Spanish. Getting this opportunity was a huge accomplishment, but one that had come at a price: he knew he was out of balance. Over time he had neglected his friendships and family as he focused on excelling in school. He was unable to internalize his accomplishments and felt like a fraud—a sensation known as impostor syndrome. Surely living abroad would slow his pace, resolve his worrisome mind, and bring him back in balance.

Budget: Funds provided by fellow Buddhist community members

Duration: Three months

Goal: To feel at home in the world again

Trigger: Despite his move abroad, it didn't take long to figure out that his habitual patterns traveled with him. Austin found himself in a space that seemed to amplify his feelings of groundlessness. He was living in a foreign land. It was hard to fit in. He was ten years older than his fellow students and a good ten to twenty years younger than his professors.

Toward the end of the first year, Austin was offered an architecture job in the nearby city of Bilbao. He jumped at the chance to work internationally in a city renowned for masterpieces by Frank Gehry, architect of the Guggenheim Museum. Yet his inner turmoil continued; he still felt not quite comfortable or convinced he belonged. Austin accepted the offer, but first he negotiated to return to the United States for one month. He wanted to connect with his missed friends and family. While in the States, Austin visited his best friend William, who had been living in a Buddhist community for two years. William invited a reluctant Austin to a ten-day meditation retreat. Why would he want to spend an entire third of his time at home in silence?

Despite his reservations, Austin attended. It was a pivotal turning point in how he felt about himself. The practice of meditating eight hours a day was surprisingly demanding. By the last day, Austin felt like he was whole again. He returned as planned to Bilbao and began to meditate daily. He committed to practicing meditation thirty minutes before work followed by about an hour of yoga. He would meditate another thirty minutes during or before a meal. On weekends he set out on the local train to the Atlantic coast, tent and sleeping bag on his back. He spent this time immersed in nature, surfing, and camping. Meditating helped him feel like a kid again. He was full of curiosity, levity, and wonder, and he felt a newfound sense of calmness and energized renewal.

Austin knew he wanted to deepen the practice of quieting the mind. After his year in Bilbao, he moved to Ojai, California, to study the Buddhist community and labor with a Buddhist building crew. It was a perfect fit: combining his craft and Buddhism.

A year and a half after his ten-day introduction to meditation, Austin was invited to a three-month "rainy season" Tibetan Buddhist meditation retreat. He felt drawn to go and knew the time would be well spent and help him further understand what was going on within him. The community covered the costs of lodging, meals, and teachings, allowing Austin to focus solely on study and practice. It was an ideal setup.

Looking back on his experience, Austin realized he'd avoided his yearnings to connect with people and his colleagues. The extreme activities he loved, such as rock climbing, were ways he avoided intimacy in relationships. Paradoxically, his attraction to the rich symbolism and nuances of Tibetan Buddhism often kept him in his cerebral mind instead of living fully in his body—he analyzed different practices instead of easing into the rawness of direct, unscripted physical experiences of meditation practice.

Plan: Spend ninety days in self-reflection, following a rigorous schedule of practice and study near Cayucos, California. This included a two-week solo retreat, followed by two weeks of kyudo practice, or Zen archery. Austin chose kyudo as a moving meditation to transition back into the world before he and his companions left the center.

One of the first talks he attended was on the Wheel of Dharma, an elaborate teaching on how individuals get stuck in habitual patterns. Austin experienced a profound moment of insight. He realized that the teaching was also about creativity. He saw how people could regain a natural creative flow by breaking habitual patterns. Over the next eight years, Austin developed this seed of insight into a book he wrote in 2012 titled *The Shoreline of Wonder: On Being Creative.*

The more he learned, the more he felt confused. His insights were stirring up all kinds of new thoughts and emotions. He was acutely aware of his emotional responses and was experiencing more feelings than ever before. He grew suspicious of his motivations, and he questioned his character and decisions. Why was he working to be an architect? What was he meant to do? What did it look like to truly feel whole and fulfilled?

Looking back, Austin realized his confusion was a necessary part of his journey. His pensive questioning helped him chip away at self-defeating patterns. His own self-questioning and reflection continues to help him to transform and shape who he is today.

Impact: The three-month Buddhist retreat changed almost every aspect of Austin's life. Before his pause, Austin was reactionary. He behaved in ways that made him feel good and emotionally safe. Now, when he loses himself in the minutiae and business of everyday life, which is all too easy to do, he knows he simply needs to reconnect with himself through meditation, prayer, singing, or some other nourishing activity. His life is workable again.

Before his pause, Austin primarily relied on his intellect to figure out next steps. Now he is guided by relegating the mind as a tool in service of the heart. Pausing permitted Austin to question his activities and examine his underlying motivations, positive and negative, while cozying up to the unknown. Only recently has he learned to embrace the wisdom from his pauses and turn it into a workable framework that helps others and supports his family. Austin has since felt less isolated and more open to challenges. He expects and accepts getting derailed sometimes, and he knows he will learn and move forward as a result of his failures, mistakes, and fiascos.

Today, Austin is a huge advocate of pauses of all sorts: from formal retreats to camping in the wilderness. He is also more in touch with his yearnings to make a difference and connect with the outside world, his community, and his family. As a founding member of 3 Lights Design, he's designed three retreat centers, including the award-winning Prana del Mar Retreat and Wellness Center in Baja, Mexico. Based on his insights about creativity and the Wheel of Dharma on his pause, Austin founded Creativity Matters in 2012. He works with individuals who want to unlock their full creative potential and organizations seeking to build cultures of innovation.

PRACTICE OF PAUSE ADVICE

It's as important to "be" as it is to "do."
Being is not only nourishing, it is also the source of creative insights. Being is at a premium in our "doer" world. Take time to experience the moment and relish it. Acknowledge your emotions and use sensory perception to take in what you feel, see, hear, touch, and taste.

You will never get to your next destination until you are able to stop and be in the place you are.
If something isn't working or you aren't happy where you are, chances are the next place you go will not bring you contentment in the long term, either. If you change your external environment, it doesn't mean your internal environment will change. It's important to make conscious changes and learn from the place you are.

Make the dark conscious.
As Carl Jung said, "One does not become enlightened by imagining figures of light, but by making the darkness conscious." The places we consciously or unknowingly avoid

or repress hold our greatest potential for growth, healing, and feeling whole and complete.

Create a vision and mission for your life.
This includes a sense of where you are going and why you are going there. It helps facilitate synchronicity, connects us to others on similar paths, and puts us in touch with those we can serve best. When things aren't going well, it helps us avoid mind-numbing distractions.

Be mindful of transitions.
Acknowledge when you are starting your workday and when you are done. Recognize when you are taking time to rest (pause) and when you are choosing to engage. If you are a parent, be fully present around your children as best you can, and if something comes up, ask them for permission to step away as needed. Our ability to start and stop activities and model those behaviors to others consciously enables us to feel engaged, enlivened, and nourished.

Practice of Pause Moments:
Chapter 6

It's important to remember how mindful following your breath can be. It's the simplest and often the most convenient tool for attention training. It's always available to you. See the instructions in chapter 1.

Try a daily mini pause or one of David King Keller's MicroMindfulness™ techniques from this chapter.

Pick one mini pause you are willing to try and practice it

within the next thirty minutes. What happens when you try it? Work up to doing one a day for a full week. Do the same one, or experiment and see what works best. Record the results of each pause in your pausebook or journal.

- Type of mini pause:
- Date and time:
- Duration:
- Level of difficulty for settling into the present moment:

   (1 = extremely hard; 2 = difficult but doable;
   3 = somewhat easy; 4 = easy/no problem)

- What did you notice, sense, feel, or think?
- What did you say or do in order to orient to the present moment?
- How did you feel before, during, or after your time for reflection?

Chapter 7

The Digital Device Pause

Human freedom involves our capacity to pause
between the stimulus and response and, in that pause, to choose the one
response toward which we wish to throw our weight.

—ROLLO MAY

WE ARE MORE CONNECTED THAN EVER. We engage in more time online than ever before, thanks to the array of digital devices available to us, twenty-four hours a day. We rely on GPS tools to get us where we need to go. We explore brands and content through all kinds of electronic means. We check in on friends via text message or social media without a voice conversation. As much as this works in our favor for many reasons, such as the advancement of medicine or technology, there is a downside.

According to the 2013 Kleiner Perkins Caufield & Byers annual Internet Trends report, on average, globally, people check their phones 150 times per day.[1] This means every two to three minutes we are interrupting our lives to check a text, e-mail, Web site, or mobile app. According to the Nielsen Total Audience Report for the first quarter of 2016, we interact with screens for more than ten hours a day, an increase of one hour over the same period in 2015.[2] Americans now own four digital devices on average, and the average U.S. consumer spends sixty hours a week consuming content across devices.[3] We have reached critical mass. Here are a few more statistics to digest:[4]

- 64 percent of overall social media users say they use social media sites at least once a day via their computer
- 47 percent of smartphone owners visit social networks every day
- 83 percent of American households have a high-definition TV (HDTV)
- 80 percent have an Internet-connected computer
- 65 percent own at least one smartphone
- 49 percent have a digital video recorder (DVR)
- 46 percent have a gaming console, adding to more media consumption overall

Nielsen reports that we live in a "two-screen minimum era: 84 percent of smartphone and tablet owners say they use their devices as second screens while watching TV at the same time."[5] Even if we're not in front of a computer at work—and many of us are—the statistics are eye-opening. Thirty-nine percent of Americans use social media while at work, and 21 percent log on to social sites while in the bathroom. Roughly one million Americans turn to social media feeds daily to discuss what's happening in the world.

You get the point. At any given time, we can conclude that a citizen of the information age spends a lot of time in front of some type of digital device, consuming media. Think about what the implications are for you, your family, society, and the world. Disconnecting on a regular basis isn't only a good idea. It's a necessity.

Did anyone realize when the first cell phones appeared how they would come to dominate our lives? I'm not implying that the use of technology is unequivocally detrimental. However, there is an addictive quality about constantly checking e-mail or the latest social media postings. In fact, they've already been grouped into a category of habits called "soft addictions," a term coined by Judith Wright, who in chapter 2 introduced us to the concept of yearnings. She reminds us that too often we confuse our yearnings with surface-level needs (recall my technology intervention, where I was pursuing surface-level needs to meet my deeper yearnings, which remained unfulfilled). In her book *The Soft Addiction Solution* Wright reports, "Without our pain available to us, we don't grasp that something profound is happening beneath the surface. We eat, shop, and watch TV in place of taking effective action. We can't feel our spiritual hunger to meet our yearning to be loved, to matter, and to make a difference."[6]

As humans, we desperately try to appease our trivial cravings with things that provide instant gratification for our egos but do not fulfill our souls' larger hungers. Soft addictions are the ordinary, everyday activities like surfing the Internet or TV, shopping, eating, and obsessing about sports, fashion, or celebrity gossip. It can also be a mood we are comfortable in and choose to be in without realizing it. For example, when I yearn to feel connected, instead of asking for a hug or making eye contact, I may resort to whining and getting attention in an indirect way. It worked as a little girl, but it doesn't fulfill me quite the same way. These soft addictions have a cost. They create barriers between ourselves and real emotional nourishment. Just like hard addictions such as gambling and drug or alcohol addiction, soft addictions need to be recognized and treated. The way to treat soft addictions is to recognize when you are indulging in them, ask yourself what your deeper yearning is, and take note of how you are feeling and fulfill those larger yearnings.

I decided to perform my own digital device audit. How preoccupied was I with technology on any given day? I did a quick inventory of my week. I found that on average, during my waking hours I had about two hours of non-digital-device time. It was usually when I was in the gym at a spin class or yoga class, or late at night when I was reading a book or journaling. That's it. Two hours. I fell right in line with the statistics.

Digital Detox

In 2013, Oxford Dictionaries defined the term *digital detox* as "a period of time during which a person refrains from using electronic devices such as smartphones or computers."[7] It is good to see this definition is officially a part of our cultural lexicon. It means the concern is widespread and we are thinking more about unplugging our digital devices.

You don't need me to tell you that most of us feel tethered to technology. I jones for digital fixes or data several times a day. Similar to when Kathleen gave me my technology intervention on my first day of pausing, I had no awareness that the innocuous little screen between me and another person was trouble. Someone needed to let me know that my behavior was not acceptable. Thankfully, I had forgiving friends who cared enough to let me know what I was doing wasn't healthy.

Today, I'm acutely aware of my addiction to my technology habits and have made an effort to shift them. If I catch myself wanting to distract myself with an e-mail—one of my favorite diversions or soft addictions—I ask myself, "What am I yearning for right now?" I may allow myself to indulge in my e-mail in-box for a few minutes, maybe longer, but I set a limit. I have boundaries for this sort of indulgence, and I realize it's likely there's something I want to avoid expressing or feeling. I tell myself, "Rachael, there you go again. You're trying to keep busy to avoid yourself, your feelings, or just being." I take a breath. I stop. I resist the temptation to check a screen. Instead I amuse myself in some way that diverts my attention. I focus on something else. I look up and listen to a conversation, put my device down, and recognize my feelings. I focus on being fully engaged in a single moment.

A digital device pause, or DDP, as I like to say, is critical in our day and age with what's becoming a normal "always on" mentality. For a digital device pause, you don't have to quit your job or travel around the world. You can do it from wherever you are, for however long you need, working within the constraints you have in your life and its demands. This type of pause is about changing how you interact with technology. You can shift how much time you spend with technology by choosing to power down for a set amount of time. What if you hit pause and spent twenty-four hours free from screens?

PAUSE STORY
Tiffany Shlain

*From Successful Media Entrepreneur
to Ritualizing the "Tech Shabbat"*

Entrepreneur and documentary filmmaker Tiffany Shlain lives in the Bay Area with her husband, Ken Goldberg, and two children. Tiffany is no stranger to technology. Her livelihood depends on it. She has created, directed, and produced numerous documentary films and has won more than seventy awards and distinctions for her work. Tiffany runs her own media company, the Moxie Institute, and a nonprofit, Let It Ripple.

Budget: Varies, but usually nothing, or just the cost of what's done in one day

Duration: Twenty-four hours, Friday sunset to Saturday sunset (Shabbat)

Goal: Ritualize the Tech Shabbat

Trigger: Tiffany was researching neuroscience for her 2011 documentary *Connected*, a film she directed and created that highlights how interconnected we are as individuals and as a society. In it, she investigates the connections between her own experiences and the world at large. Tiffany began to see how disconnecting from technology would benefit her busy lifestyle.

Tiffany's father was also suffering from brain cancer at this time, which is well documented in *Connected*. Tiffany came up with the idea for a "Tech Shabbat," a ritual of digitally disconnecting one day a week, after her father passed away. Creating this type of pause was a natural next step to build a ritual break from technology into her daily and weekly routine. Tiffany recalls, "Losing my father was a wake-up call. What are we doing with the people we love, if we are only here for a short time?"

Tiffany named it in honor of the Jewish traditional Shabbat practiced to celebrate the holy day of rest. It is interesting to note that the actual day, Saturday, isn't what is considered holy—it's in recognition of God's day of rest during the Creation. Orthodox Jews who practice Shabbat also do not use any technology during this time. They go a step further and don't use cars, lights, or anything electronic or mechanical, including some routines most of us wouldn't give a second thought to, such as taking an elevator. No matter how extreme you decide to go, why not dedicate one day in recognition of rest and reflect on all you have to be grateful for or spend time with friends and family?

Plan: In Hebrew, both the words "sabbatical" and "Shabbat" stem from the same root word, Sabbath. Sabbath literally means "a ceasing"—a rest from work, or a break; it's often thought of as one day, but occasionally refers to longer periods of time. It is fitting that Tiffany's sabbatical occurs on the actual day of the Sabbath, Saturday, in the traditional Jewish practice.

This ritual of unplugging one day a week, for twenty-four hours, has taken on significance in Tiffany's family. As she explains, "Just having one day with no screens or interruptions feels so refreshing." Tiffany, her husband, and her two kids have made it into a way to spend more family time together. During this time, they create a beautiful meal and take the opportunity to express what they are grateful for before eating together. As a family, they feel more connected to each other. As individuals, they feel more connected to themselves.

As Tiffany explains in her TED Book, *Brain Power: From Neurons to Networks*, "The idea is to utilize one of the best features on your favorite tech device, the Off Switch."[8] The day is typically spent outside with friends, family, or nature. Sometimes there are art projects. Other times there's plenty of engaging in activities or discussions. There are no rules to follow, except that devices stay off. Sometimes it feels like multiple days are compressed into twenty-four hours.

The only exception happens when Tiffany travels or is speaking at a conference. This doesn't happen often, maybe a few times a year. Otherwise she sticks to the plan.

During Tiffany's Tech Shabbat, the biggest challenge lies in making plans with other people. In a day and age when people expect that you can receive e-mail or always get a text message, this is difficult. Getting places without a GPS or phone navigation system keeps things simple and pre-Internet era—directions and maps are printed out in advance. The household landline phone is kept alive for Saturdays in case people need to get in touch or for an emergency. Although in the nearly six years of their Tech Shabbats, there has hardly been a need to use it.

Impact: Tiffany feels refreshed, rejuvenated, and ready to appreciate the Internet anew every time she returns from a Tech Shabbat. It's so easy to take things for granted with technology and the Internet at our fingertips. Not only is Tiffany more grateful, she feels more creative. She created one of the most helpful infographics I've come across to help others plan their own Tech Shabbat and understand its benefits. You can view it online at www.moxieinstitute.org/technology_shabbats.

PRACTICE OF PAUSE ADVICE

We all love the Internet, but anything that you do too much is not a good thing.
If you find yourself glued to your devices, or a little too dependent on them, try a Tech Shabbat and see how you feel.

Experience the positive ripple effect of taking a Tech Shabbat.
If you start a Tech Shabbat, chances are others may follow suit. On Saturdays Tiffany's staff know she is taking a break. She encourages all of them to unplug and take their own version for themselves.

The Sleep Detox

More than 30 percent of us don't get enough sleep, says Arianna Huffington in her bestselling book *Thrive*, citing the Centers for Disease Control and Prevention.[9] Among other sleep tips, she suggests making the bedroom a digital-device-free zone. For her New Year's resolution, she committed to thirty days with a goal of eight hours of sleep a night. Many factors led to her success, including keeping devices out of the bedroom. She kept her multiple devices, she writes, "charging far, far away from my bed, to help me avoid the middle-of-the-night temptation to check the latest news or latest emails."[10] (I'd suggest adding the bathroom to the device-free zone list.)

- Avoid having devices in your bedroom during or before bedtime. You are less likely to check them first thing when you wake up or respond to an incoming phone call or message after bedtime.

■ Avoid using any screen for at least ninety minutes before bedtime. In July 2015, *Digital Trends* published an article on how the particular spectrum of blue light emitted by your devices affects your quantity and quality of sleep. That particular spectrum of light, says Michael J. Breus, a clinical psychologist and sleep therapist, "sends a signal to an area of the brain known as the suprachiasmatic nucleus and tells it to turn off melatonin production. Melatonin is the key that starts the engine for sleep." Breus adds, "There's nothing wrong with blue light for most of the day. You just don't want to have it about 90 minutes or so before bed."[11]

The Extended Detox

■ Select one day a week or a month to go without any device use. For example, create a rule that Saturdays are Digital Device Pause Day. Sound daunting? All the more reason to try it.

■ Establish specific times of day that are technology free, like from 7:00 to 8:00 p.m., or mealtimes. Collect cell phones and place them in a stack during this time (a great help to those who have urges to check them).

■ Create a stretch of thirty days where nothing is used to connect, other than human contact or your analog voice (no e-mail or social media).

■ Set up a digital-free room, such as your bedroom, where no cell phones, TV, or tablets are ever allowed. That means charging happens outside of this room, too.

Decide what you can tolerate, and it should feel like a stretch. Paradoxically, you can live a more personally connected life by choosing to disconnect from your devices. It may take a little experimenting, but you can find what works and take a digital detox.

Take the Digital Device Pause Challenge: Unplug for One Day

Just like Tiffany, you can pause from technology—even if it's for one day. One way is to join the annual National Day of Unplugging (NDU). This is similar to Tiffany's Tech Shabbat, but is its own movement, a project of Reboot, a nonprofit whose mission is to create "vital, resonant and meaningful Jewish experiences" (but you don't have to be Jewish to participate!). It is globally recognized every year on the first weekend of March. Participants decide to what extreme to unplug. Some people go all out and do not use any electricity, including heat or power. Others refrain from accessing any entertainment, Internet, or other communications at work or home. The spectrum is wide. To me this sounds like the perfect excuse to plan a camping trip. Post pictures, print out a sign, and state why you're unplugging—read more about it at nationaldayofunplugging.com.

Going to miss this day, or don't want to wait for it to come around again? Pick any day or amount of time and unplug. Reboot also has a mobile app, called Friday, available on the Apple iTunes store. Friday offers a warm welcome and helps you begin to unwind thirty minutes before sunset. Whatever you decide to do, I recommend starting with just one day, or even a part of your day. This means turning off your cell

phone and getting off the grid. What better excuse to get outdoors for a hike, read a real book with paper pages, or connect
with friends? All of these are great ways to spend your unplugged time.

It requires some planning to set yourself up for success.
Unless you live under a rock at Retreat Road, you probably
will have some interactions with technology. Decide what
you are willing to do without during your detox. One of the
most important parts of an unplugged pause is reflecting afterward on how it affected you. Did you identify and fulfill a
yearning like connecting in person, instead of texting over
the phone? You may notice that taking action, or engaging to
satisfy a yearning, works better *without* the use of technology.
You can begin planning your technology-free pause using the
journal prompts in the Practice of Pause Moments at the end
of this chapter.

Again, a pause can happen anytime, anywhere. What matters is making the most of your time. A pause is your gateway
to change what you do or how you think by shifting your
behavior.

Pauses aren't just about recharging. Whether it's a digital
device pause or one deep, conscious breath, a pause gives you
permission to think differently. It is a chance to shift your behavior and sink deeply into yourself. It is an opportunity to
practice deep listening to yourself. These different types of
pauses may prompt you to investigate something inside of
you. They may trigger a response you least expected or spark
a new idea. They may be filled with fear about what you may
discover about yourself. This is an opportunity to lean into
that fear, and trust yourself and its outcome.

PAUSE STORY
Danielle LaPorte

*From Digital Diva to Digital-Free "Sprucing and Juicing"
and Creativity Genesis*

If you haven't yet come across Danielle LaPorte, you haven't experienced one of the most influential, consciously minded, inspirational writers of our time. When we crossed paths in 2011, Danielle was already a big success and was living her dream of helping others reach their goals as an author, speaker, and motivational diva. Since this was my first encounter with Danielle, I felt fortunate as I settled in to hear her speak in a hot, sweaty church at the World Domination Summit hosted by Chris Guillebeau, the *New York Times* bestselling author of *The Art of Non-Conformity*, *The $100 Startup*, and *Born for This*.

A church seemed fitting for the World Domination Summit, where I heard Danielle deliver her message about how to be true to yourself and how each of us possesses the desires and capabilities to be creative and produce magnificence. At the time, her first book, *The Fire Starter Sessions*, had been published and was climbing its way up the *New York Times* bestseller list.

Budget: Nothing beyond normal living expenses

Duration: One month

Goal: To pause, and for her staff to pause, for one month to replenish creative juices and get ready to embark on the next book and project

Trigger: Danielle lives and breathes what she preaches—creative integrity. To optimize her creative spirit, voice, and intention, that means recharging her batteries every so often. It can mean plain checking out. *The Fire Starter Sessions* was officially finished and launched. It was time to recharge. Danielle felt the need to unwind and knew that if she gave herself downtime to slow down and disconnect, her creativity would benefit all the more. She wanted to take her creativity to the next level once she returned. Danielle decided that a digital pause from the outside world was just what she needed.

Plan: For one month, Danielle would deprioritize technology. She banned her use of digital devices and the Internet and went on hiatus from devices for the month. Her whole team would do the same. For a digital diva like Danielle, who built her career and following through online media, this was a bold move. She still watched some TV, but overall she made the call that no cell phone activity, social media, video updates, blogging, e-mails, or anything else would happen on her digital hiatus. She let the world know in a blog post. Just like that, she was over and out.

Impact: Two weeks into her digital pause, Danielle became more aware of her creative rhythm. Her idea to go on hiatus was working. She returned to work refreshed, renewed, and energized to take on whatever came next. She soon began working on her next book, *The Desire Map*, for those who want to create lasting change in their lives; it was published two years later and became a best seller.

PRACTICE OF PAUSE ADVICE

Recharge your batteries completely.
Do this whenever and however you can. To borrow Danielle's wise analogy, you can extend the life of rechargeable batteries by charging them up fully instead of constantly using

half-charged batteries. Over the long term, batteries that are allowed to fully charge up are more durable and last longer.

Remember that everything is energy.
Everything. Have intention with how you spend your time. When Danielle first announced her pause in her blog, she recognized this and wrote, "This space, which I think of as my digital temple, or laboratory, has its own energy and vibration. All life force needs to wax and wane. The engine needs to cool."

Realize whatever you think, do, or feel matters.
Do not waste your energy; use it in ways you feel are worth your time, inspire you, or allow you to create something. Your own energy imprint will be on whatever you do.

Practice of Pause Moments:
Chapter 7

What's one way you can shift your media habits and/or consumption to improve your sleep quality?

What would your digital device pause plan look like starting this week?

How would you hold yourself accountable?

Chapter 8

The Extended Pause

I am not in this world to live up to other people's expectations,
nor do I feel that the world must live up to mine.

—FRITZ PERLS

IF YOU ARE one of the lucky people like me who work for an employer that allows extended leaves of absence or time off, paid or unpaid, congratulations! The first step is to determine what options are available for your pause. What does your employer offer? Or what is possible in terms of an extended vacation?

If you can swing it, whether because your company offers some kind of extended leave or you've managed to save up enough vacation days for a nice long break, an extended pause will give you a prime opportunity to recharge and reconnect with yourself. Nonprofit research company WorldatWork surveyed more than five thousand members about paid time off in 2016. The report found that fewer organizations (10 percent) are offering sabbaticals, whether paid or partially paid (4 percent) or unpaid (6 percent), as compared to the number of firms that did in both 2010 (15 percent) and 2014 (14 percent).

When taking a sabbatical leave, 46 percent of companies require that employees further their education as part of their leave and that the skills be related to their current employer or job, while 43 percent have no requirements for employees taking sabbatical leave.[1] In addition to these companies, nineteen of those listed among *Fortune* magazine's 2016 Top 100 Best Companies to Work For offer sabbatical benefits.[2]

From this data it appears that even with increasing demands in the modern workplace, the trends for offering extended leave are unfortunately on the decline. It is up to us as individuals in these corporations to ensure we are getting the renewal we need even if our companies don't offer a formal extended leave program. That is why learning how to pause is so important no matter what your time limitations are.

For my three months, I didn't want to do anything other than spend time with myself and figure out what to do next in my career. I fantasized about traveling to new continents. Maybe I would go to faraway lands or visit old friends. I wanted the freedom to pick up and go anywhere. But thinking through my options, I knew that, more than anything else, I needed downtime. I was not up for planning a trip that required lots of prep work. I dreaded planning anything. This included deciding if I should get out of bed in the morning and return to work. I was too burned out to do anything other than just show up.

What I didn't realize was that the power of taking a pause is in the ability to show up for it. Sometimes, showing up is the best thing you can do. It's not easy to make the call that you want to change something or shift your behavior. We are also governed by our limbic system deep inside our brains. Sometimes referred to as the "mammalian brain," its job is to create not only our basic drives but also our emotions, and to constantly evaluate those states.[3] Our limbic brains want to keep us safe and out of harm's way. Change usually means doing something unfamiliar, which can bring about anxiety and inertia. Limbic brain alarm bells may start sounding, warning you not to go into the unknown. Know and expect this type of resistance from your brain. After all, it's how your ancestors survived and how you got here.

As already discussed in chapter 3, you don't have to have everything figured out before you pause. By not planning, you allow your pause to take on an adventurous, therapeutic, magical quality. Your circuitry can change when you allow yourself time to think or to step away from your previous habits. There's no obligation to follow any set plan, create a big plan, or have any plan, for that matter. On the outside, pausing may look irresponsible if there is no grandiose plan, and the common perception may be that the pauser is being a slacker. But actually, not planning leads to less overthinking, and overthinking is frequently why many people need to "zone out" or take a pause in the first place. Showing up without a plan is the most helpful thing you can do for yourself in a crisis of overconnectedness or mental hardship.

Maximizing Your Time Off When Funded by Your Employer

Not only is it rare to find any firm that supports extended leaves, it's extremely uncommon to work at a company that is among the 4 percent that offer extended paid time off. If you are one of the fortunate ones working at a company that offers this, here is how to make the best use of it.

First, there are a few challenges to consider as you embark

on a leave of absence. These include deciding what to do with your time, figuring out how it will be financed, communicating your plans to others, and guaranteeing that your job will be there for you when you return (assuming you still want it).

For a paid pause, usually the company sets the maximum time frame. This is typically documented in company policy and subject to manager approval. It's common that you'll need to have been an employee of the company for several years (often five to ten) to qualify for a paid leave.

If corporations offer paid sabbaticals, what is the incentive to return? When I left DoubleClick to spend time traveling to New Zealand and Australia for a four-week period (a company perk at the time was four weeks of time off after five years of employment), I was overjoyed that my company offered this benefit. I valued a company that allowed time to leave and replenish. The last thing on my mind was to quit and not return. It turns out, I'm in the majority.

In December 2015, I surveyed 235 Internet users and asked, "How likely would you be to return to the same job if you took an unpaid leave of time off?" Like me, 58 percent of respondents said they would either absolutely return (37 percent) or probably return (21 percent). Another 26 percent said that they wouldn't take any time off even if offered. Fourteen percent said they would not return.

When I asked, "If your current job offered unpaid time off in addition to standard vacation, how much time would you take off?" 30 percent of respondents would decline taking the time off even if offered, but 23 percent would take a week off and 18 percent would take a month off.[4]

So what does this tell us? In my small sample of results, those who would want to take a pause, even if it was one week, would self-select and do so if it was offered. The majority of employees would return to their place of employment. Employees could use their unpaid leave in a way that worked for them. Companies could offer it as an additional perk and have happier, more satisfied employees, knowing they are trusted to return after taking an unpaid leave.

I recommend timing your pause so it includes holiday dates to maximize your time off. If you happen to be able to work for a few days or a week remotely from a different city or country and your boss is okay with that, do so. The knowledge economy can be flexible and it's at least worth asking what is possible. The change in scenery and work environment, and the potential for adventure, can quench your thirst for new stimuli and create new experiences and neural pathways. At the same time, your limbic brain's anxiety is at ease knowing you are saving vacation days (and adding more pause days wherever you are). If your company policy allows, you may even be able to take an additional week of vacation to extend your trip where you are. This is a gift, and if you can do it, go for it.

In my case, during my 2004 pause, I landed in Sydney after two weeks in New Zealand. I worked out of the Sydney office for four days catching up on e-mails and taking next steps for a few important projects. Then I took a standard week of vacation. My time off extended from the standard four weeks to six weeks with relative ease. I traveled to the Gold Coast north of Sydney. I hopped from hostel to hostel on my way up to the azure waters of the Whitsunday Islands, one of the most beautiful and memorable highlights of my trip.

My Extended Pause Plan

Fast-forward to Google, 2011. While I was still working, I started crafting my plan. I committed to doing a few mini trips, leaving the rest of my time open and unplanned. I had no idea if I'd return to Google after three months or continue to pause. What I did know was that I'd start with the three months I had and trusted I would figure it out at some point.

Mini trip 1: Visit my younger brother, Drew, in Austin, Texas, for one week

Mini trip 2: Spend recuperation time in the Sierra Nevada

Mini trip 3: Burning Man

For anyone who is not familiar with Burning Man, it is a seven-day festival that takes place in the Black Rock Desert in Nevada. More than seventy thousand people gathered for it in 2016. It is an ideal opportunity to pause and intentionally shift your behavior. There's no electricity or Internet, and most people find themselves quickly out of their comfort zone—it is described as "an experiment in radical self-reliance and located in one of the most inhospitable spots on the planet."[5] What better environment to pause from everyday life was there? It was out of my comfort zone and required intentionally shifting my behavior to this new culture and environment.

I didn't decide to go to Burning Man until about halfway through my extended pause. The annual festival in the Nevada desert coincided with the last week of my three-month leave. It was the same week as my thirty-ninth birthday. Each time I thought about it I shrugged it off. Camping was camping, after all, and why would I bother to do it with so many people in a hot, noisy, uncomfortable environment? How much different could it be?

How wrong I was. Saying yes to Burning Man opened me to new opportunities and different ways of doing *and* being I would not have experienced otherwise. I realized that there were so many other ways to live that I hadn't even considered before. I met people who continue to affect my life in meaningful ways. It became another door I walked through during my pause. Burning Man helped me see that everyone has a creative, curious, and playful side that can be tapped into and developed. This perspective remained with me long after I left the desert.

Burning Man took my pause to a new level. Over the course of the six days, I became more aware of who I was becoming. I was clearer without the distractions of everyday life. I was surrounded by inspiring, bigger-than-life art installations, impromptu musical concerts and DJs, and people who were also living in the moment, full of presence and life.

My experience at Burning Man introduced me to a new goal: to be present, engaged, and connected with those with whom I interacted. Traveling to a new destination created an urgency to live in the moment in my everyday life. Burning Man influenced my entire job search. I learned new skills and ways to adapt and connect with others that influenced my job search over the twelve weeks that followed. I never would have had this "aha" moment if I had adhered to a rigid schedule during my pause. Allow yourself the same flexibility to be open to new experiences and opportunities.

Managing Your Time

There is an irony to having too much spare time. It is easy to get overwhelmed by how much time is suddenly available, which can cause paralysis to do or plan anything. Going from a structure of fixed work hours and routine to no structure is difficult. Remember, most brains love and crave structure and routine, especially if that is what you are accustomed to.

What will your plan look like? Not knowing or planning all the details allows for the unexpected. Remember to keep it simple. Whatever your plan, make sure you include some downtime for self-care. By this, I don't mean going to the spa or treating yourself to a movie or new clothes. I'm talking about radical self-care. More on this in chapter 10, "Tips for a Meaningful Pause."

Focus on Quality and Presence

Pausing is an ideal time to be more present. You don't have to rush into the next thing or check something off a list. It's an opportunity to find out how you feel in the moment, to be present to yourself and whatever task is at hand. If I learned nothing else from my three months off, it was how to focus on the *quality* of life in any given moment, not the *quantity* of what I was doing. It is a chance to avoid going through the motions, and instead connect and engage in new ways. Make eye contact with your coffee barista. Call a friend you haven't talked to in months who has crossed your mind. Smile at strangers while walking down the street. What will you see? What will you experience? Think of your pause as your playground.

Pausing is also an ideal opportunity to reflect. Write about what you feel and what you experience in your journal or pausebook. It is a great way to process your experiences and document what matters to you. Writing can be a way to integrate your new routines and behavior norms. You can savor and deepen your experiences.

Journaling is also a good exercise in being present (along with being a power tool, as discussed in chapter 3.). Judith Blackstone, author of *Belonging Here: A Guide for the Spiritually Sensitive Person*, created a step-by-step guide to help readers be more here and now with what she calls the "Realization Process."[6] This process leverages an individual's innate physical and spiritual gifts. Blackstone makes the point that each of us can use our spiritual gifts as entryways into both the depths of human connection and our innermost selves. When you tap into this, your physical presence and engagement with others deepens.

I'm reminded of Ram Dass, author of the 1971 classic *Be Here Now, Remember*. I had no idea who Ram Dass was during my extended pause, but what he wrote helps me see that I was cultivating self-compassion by being with myself at any given moment. I wasn't thinking about the next box to check, or worrying if someone thought I was doing well at my job. Ram Dass writes:

> *Just be here now. Reflect on the thought that if you are truly Here and Now—a) it is enough, and b) you will have optimum power and understanding to do the best thing at the given moment. Thus when "then" (the future) becomes Now—if*

you have learned this discipline—you will then be in an ideal position to do the best thing. So you need not spend your time worrying about then.[7]

So what does it take to shift? Start with a conscious breath. Take a good inventory of your limiting beliefs and apply the mental TASERing technique. What limiting beliefs and rules exist that are shaping your present-day behavior? What new belief or intention can you create instead? The more you practice, the more you can shift.

Find the Pause Magic

How often are we oblivious to what is happening around us until we stop or change course? By design, an extended pause is a chance to discover new ways of being and stay curious about others and yourself. It's an opportunity to take inventory of your motives and thoughts and the choices you make. You can set an intention to become more aware of your own feelings and deepen your emotional intelligence skill set, which requires conscious effort. This requires daily mental flossing and TASERing. In an extended pause, you have more time to play with and notice how you act, think, and feel over the course of several weeks or more. With the gift of an extended pause you can try something new each day, incorporate journaling as a daily ritual, or set ongoing time aside to focus on how you want to shift and take actions to make it happen.

One of the benefits of pausing and being more present is that I feel more in my body and aware of my emotions. An extended pause allows more time to shift into a new mindset. A weekend pause, and going back to work after it, is still a benefit, but what if you spent multiple days, weeks, or months immersing yourself in a new way of being? Having more time means increasing the likelihood for new habits to form while old ways of being fade away. Without the usual stimuli around, experiencing something new creates new neural networks, which over time lead to new thoughts and behaviors. What will you discover in the extended pause magic that you may have missed before?

Communicating Before and During an Extended Pause

A frequent question I heard while planning or during my pause was, "So, what are you going to do now?" It drove me crazy. If you are taking an extended pause, don't be surprised if you get a similar question.

> *"What's next for you?"*
> *"Do you have a game plan once you are done?"*
> *"Why are you doing this?"*
> *"Are you going to go back to work?"* (My personal favorite.)

In each instance, an awkward silence typically ensued. It didn't matter if I was at a cocktail party talking to complete strangers or having a conversation with my mother. In time my response evolved from "I don't know yet; I'll have to see" to a sincere and honest conversation about what I wanted to express, and how I didn't know what lay ahead for me. Eventually, my answer gave rise to engaging, transformative conversations about aligning with what mattered to me and what I needed to figure out while standing still for a while.

Chances are you will field similar questions before and during your pause. Don't be caught off guard or hide from others' curiosity. Instead, shed your defenses, and choose your growth mindset. It is an invitation to share your experiences, how you feel, what you yearn for, and what you are learning or doing differently. Be a savvy communicator. Prepare and equip yourself with a few sentences to minimize stress around what you want to share. I recommend crafting a few stock answers to stay at ease and that keep you honest. Examples may include admitting you don't have an answer yet or have your next steps figured out. You can share an update if you are "looking into" or "exploring" an idea you have, and talk a little about your experience. You may feel a wave of fear or anxiety every time you share your story. Be authentic and share what naturally comes up for you. Trust that by expressing your truths you are moving closer toward your alignment.

PAUSE STORY
Ken Altmann

*From Corporate Sales Executive to
Redesigning Life on New Terms*

In 2009, Ken Altmann was a successful sales manager at Yahoo! One night Ken, his fiancée, Hillary, and another couple went out to have a few beers after work. The four good friends sat down and began catching up with each other. As the conversation continued, they hit upon a fascinating topic. What if they all quit their jobs immediately and traveled the world? What would happen? What kinds of experiences would they have? They were intoxicated with the wonder and possibility of such a dramatic shift. Was it possible? Could it be done? Did they want to give it a try?

Budget: $35,000 each (Ken and Hillary)

Duration: One year

Goal: Travel around the world, going like a local, and discover life outside of corporate America

Trigger: The seed was planted, and the more Ken thought about it, the more he realized he could make it happen with a little planning and saving. A few weeks later, Ken's friends found out they were expecting twins. They were out of the game. Hillary remained interested. It was now up to Ken if it was going to happen. He mulled over the idea some more.

Ken hadn't taken more than one week off at a time throughout his entire career. He had felt pressure not to take long holidays: it was all part of the start-up mentality that had become a standard for many young people serious about their careers. Ken had built his career working for various start-ups and was now in a great position at his current job in sales. He hadn't taken all of his vacation days in his current role, either. Now, he wanted to take 365 days off.

Hillary was a business consultant and knew that if they were to get serious about travel, they needed to step it up and start planning and saving ASAP. Both of them had similar travel goals: travel like locals, and experience life across the globe. To test out the idea, Ken and Hillary went to Australia for two weeks. Both were still working and long overdue for a vacation. Ken embraced his time away, knowing every moment counted, and he was writing his own script to follow. He didn't want to go home.

Their short Australia trip helped them take the next step: leave their jobs and travel the world for an extended period of time. Hillary and Ken made a plan: take a year off to travel the world and "leave the rat race." They spent six months planning their wedding, and they each gave six months' notice at their jobs. What better time to travel than an extended year-long honeymoon?

Plan: Now that they were engaged and had a rough timeline, the next step was critical: figuring out where to start and where to visit. One night, they taped a world map to the wall, examining all the possibilities. Everywhere was an option. They made a game out of it. Each of them got three pins to stick anywhere they wanted to prioritize. Each of them also got three "veto" votes that could negate a pin on the map.

The strategy was simple: don't overplan. Their goal was always to live like locals wherever they went. Ken and Hillary often booked flights from one country or continent to the next not knowing what they would do when they got there. To help save money and meet their "live like locals" goal, they used hostels and trains as often as possible. On one particular local train in India, Ken ripped his shorts on a jagged edge of metal, leaving them looking more like tattered rags than shorts. A stranger smiled at his appearance and said, "Welcome to India!" The kind stranger invited them to his winery and they accepted the invite, getting a taste of local life they otherwise wouldn't have had. No matter where they went, they embraced similar opportunities and tried to go with the flow whenever possible.

As Ken and Hillary continued traveling, they established a rhythmic ebb and flow. Uncertainty became so common that it wasn't something to worry about after a while. In fact, the opposite happened, and they found themselves embracing un-certainty. It no longer was a fear, but a freedom they wel-comed. It was a new way to live for both of them.

Impact: Their one-year pause, or "the Trip," as Ken and Hillary affectionately call it, changed their values and per-spectives on life forever. The most obvious evidence is that they decided to adopt a baby boy after their visit to Africa. After spending one month there, they fell in love with this part of the world and its people.

They decided to look for jobs again to replenish their bank accounts. They knew employment was mandatory to start the adoption process, for both savings and job security. Ken re-turned to online sales, and Hillary found a new job in business consulting. They didn't think they would return to corporate America, yet here they were, holding positions similar to what they had before. Even though *what* they did hadn't changed, *how* they did it had. They knew they were working to support a lifestyle that was fulfilling. They were working so they could raise a baby they hoped to soon have. They began the adoption process. To their delight, Ken and Hillary were matched with a boy from Uganda. After their travels, both feel they are better prepared as parents.

PRACTICE OF PAUSE ADVICE

Travel like a local as much as possible.
It is the best way to experience different cultures and gain new perspectives that affect how you will live the rest of your life. If you can travel like you have no money, or if you don't have much, even better. You may have to rely on others to get where you need to go or learn about an area.

The happiest people in the world are often not the richest but those with a strong sense of community.
While driving to a safari in rural Africa, Ken stopped at the town he and Hillary were to stay at that evening. Mud huts were everywhere, and there was no electricity or running water in town. They found the entire village's inhabitants gathered in one hut, dancing and singing in a Friday night ritual. They were warmly welcomed. "This is what happiness is," Ken fondly recalls.

Life is a choice, and you pull the trigger.
Life is full of scary decisions. If you take more risk, or go outside your comfort zone, it may lead to outcomes never imagined. Anyone can travel, or change something about his or her life. It sometimes requires trusting the process and letting go of control. Ken says, "I have no more courage than the next person, but I did make a decision, an unconventional one." Even with a budget near zero, there's always a way to travel if you keep needs to a minimum.

Practice of Pause Moments:
Chapter 8

Answer the following questions in your journal or pausebook—using the present tense, as if you were already in an extended pause.

Envision your ideal extended pause and describe your experience.

How do you feel?

How do you spend your time and when is it taken?

What are your intentions and in what ways do you plan to shift during this time?

How long will your extended pause last?

What are you grateful for on this extended pause?

How do you stay present during this extended pause?

Chapter 9

Creating Your Pause Playground

*He . . . who can no longer pause to wonder and stand rapt in awe,
is as good as dead; his eyes are closed.*

—ALBERT EINSTEIN

THE BEST WAY WE LEARN, like children in a playground, is through engaging in the act of play. Your pause is another version of this playground no matter how long or short, digital or analog, or how familiar or new the environment is. Feel free to experiment, test your abilities, seize opportunities, go outside your comfort zone, and have fun. Isn't that what play is all about? This chapter is about creating a pause playground that adds value for you, and you'll see how pausing is an investment in yourself no matter what the circumstances are. Included are some additional types of pauses to consider in your playground.

One of those less-than-ideal circumstances is when there's no paycheck during a pause, such as with a job layoff or while taking extended time off to parent a child. Other occasions include a period of time for a career transition, or adopting a new way of thinking about something. In all of these instances, even though there is no monetary paycheck, that doesn't mean you're not investing in yourself by pausing. Your pause can still address how you *feel* versus what you actually *do*. Once you figure out how to direct your pause and focus on the quality of your attention and intention, your well-being may dramatically shift as you become more present.

The Well-Being Payoff of Pausing

When you intentionally pause, you are receiving a kind of payoff that's very different from a financial one. You are benefiting from a payoff in emotional well-being. Taking a pause is like writing a paycheck to your soul. You are paying yourself with nonmonetary values like life lessons, quality time, insights, and deeper connection to yourself that allow you to lead and live a life that's more meaningful based on what you find out about yourself. Isn't that payoff substantial in itself?

Another way to think about emotional payoffs of pausing is when you pause to choose a different life or career path. These types of pauses generally fall into the category of non-financially-compensated pauses, including:

- Leaving a job voluntarily.
- Leaving a job involuntarily. I put this into this category because even if you receive severance, you can fund your pause partially or consider it disposable income and choose to put it toward your pause budget.

- Pursuing a new career. This could be a new job in the same field, a job in a new field, or starting a business.
- Going back to school to complete or start a degree.
- Experiencing a major life change. It may be starting a family, parental leave, returning to work, change in a relationship, or a move (geographically speaking or any other move, for that matter).
- Dealing with a change in health for yourself or a loved one. (This may or may not be paid depending on your employment circumstances.)

Regardless of how you got here, you find yourself with time off. You are the rainmaker.

If you are like the majority who do not get paid to take time off, don't worry. With a little planning you will be on your way to a purposeful pause. You may have a plan to reenter the workforce, but make sure you give yourself permission to pause. Eventually you can push the play button and start focusing on other things, like earning income or beginning a job search. Meanwhile, know that through pausing, you can turn obstacles into opportunities. It is your playground and you can play by your rules, engage, and follow your yearnings.

The Pause Paycheck

What if a pause were a way you paid yourself? Most people think about getting paid as a paycheck from an employer. Let's reframe this idea. Your pause is an investment in your spirit to replenish yourself and invigorate your livelihood. It's a way to pay it forward and reignite the spark in your life. This can happen with (preferably) or without a paycheck. Either way, it is an investment in who you are becoming. Whether your pause is long or short, you are funding a more important endeavor. You are connecting and giving yourself permission to listen to your inner voice. Pausing from your everyday activities allows you to keep out of your standard routine and focus on yourself. Know that you are cutting a check for an alternative type of payment that you write yourself—a paycheck to your soul. By taking a pause you are paying yourself with time, space, solitude, and inner focus. I don't mean to discount (pun intended) the need for an actual paycheck by an employer. It's important to keep this in mind as you assess the options available to you. Just because you aren't getting paid by your employer to take time off, or you're not getting paid at all, that doesn't mean you're not investing in yourself.

The Forced Pause

At first, a layoff may seem like a huge blow. You didn't make the grade. Your services are no longer needed for reasons beyond your control, such as budget cuts, downsizing, or a change in business strategy. No one wants to go through updating a résumé or endlessly networking to find a new job. The idea of going without a paycheck or living unemployed for any period of time is scary to a lot of people, me included.

However, this may be an eye-opening chance to find something more suitable or to take on a new challenge. Even though it's difficult to absorb sudden or unexpected news, a layoff could be the best thing that ever happens to you. With a layoff, you have an opportunity to start over. You can explore new roles or look for a new job. You are liberated to finally shift your career or reflect on what you *authentically* want to do. Maybe it gives you some time to be with your family and loved ones. You will likely discover it has benefits that you would not have predicted. In hindsight, you may find they are benefits that could have come about only as a result of this event.

Taking a pause after exiting a job can benefit you even if it's temporarily painful. This "forced pause" allows you to think through your next steps with more focus on yourself.

PAUSE STORY
Joe Kutchera

From Media Maven to Independent Consultant and Author

There is no escaping it: getting laid off stinks. Nevertheless, Joe Kutchera credits his two forced pauses as chapters where he embraced curiosity as well as a passion for writing, marketing, speaking Spanish, and Latin American culture. These two pauses pushed Joe to look within himself, overcome his fear, and, after much reflection, emerge with a renewed identity and career aspirations.

Budget: Unknown (not tracked)

Duration: Sixteen and twenty-four months, respectively

Goal: Assess next steps and career path

First Pause Trigger: In June 2009, during the thick of the financial crisis, Joe was suddenly laid off from ContextWeb, a digital advertising exchange based in New York City. He had no backup plan. His summer became an emotional roller coaster: some days it was exhilarating, with the freedom to pursue his dreams, while other days were full of anxiety, uncertainty, and shame for not having steady work or a relationship. Insomnia ensued.

Plan 1: While working in Mexico two years previously, Joe had started writing about digital media and marketing for a daily trade publication. Using that prior experience, he began contributing articles to MediaPost (a media, marketing, and advertising Web site with a larger audience), writing about a new area of expertise: U.S. Hispanic marketing. While attending the 2009 South by Southwest (SXSW) Conference, Joe sat in on a session called "How to Write Your Own Book" and felt inspired to weave a book together based on his column. He silently set a goal for himself: to write a book in the next five years.

Joe crashed on a friend's couch in Chicago to cut costs. He signed a contract to publish his book and wrote the manuscript for *Latino Link: Building Brands Online with Hispanic Communities and Content* the following year. In the meantime, the postcrisis job market proved challenging to find paying work. Again and again, the applications and interviews yielded rejections or just complete silence. Joe was not the only MBA with bilingual skills and a charming smile. He felt defeated. Yet the rejections meant Joe could continue writing his book and building his personal brand via his industry articles.

Joe never intended to take a pause. About 70 percent of his time was spent writing and the other 30 percent he spent searching for a new career. He calls this his "blended pause." Probably the hardest aspect, emotionally speaking, was receiving unemployment insurance. It deteriorated his self-confidence, being a type-A, go-getter, goal-oriented person. It proved difficult for Joe to accept not earning money for a while.

In advance of *Latino Link* coming out in the fall of 2010, Joe organized a book tour, speaking at conferences, companies, and universities across the United States. Fox News Latino and the *Huffington Post* invited Joe to contribute to their Web sites, further establishing Joe as an expert in the media.

During his book tour, Joe met Roberto Orci, the CEO of Acento Advertising. He invited Joe to organize a digital marketing workshop at his advertising agency in December 2011. The session evolved into a full-time opportunity to work at the Los Angeles agency as its director of digital media. Joe traded in a chilly Chicago for the sunshine and palm trees of Southern California. What wasn't to like?

Second Pause Trigger: The position started well enough, but when the agency lost a few clients, it eliminated a number of positions, including Joe's. Joe was hired back as a contractor, and Acento became his first client on what turned into his "consulting" career path.

Plan 2: This time around, Joe felt more positive. He looked for work and continued to write for Fox News Latino and the *Huffington Post*. A few colleagues in Hispanic marketing suggested that he write a Spanish-language version of *Latino Link* to further highlight his expertise. Taking their advice, he went to Guadalajara, Mexico, to attend the largest book fair for the Spanish-language publishing market. After a few lunches and some negotiations, Editorial Patria, part of the Hachette Book Group, signed Joe and two coauthors to write *E-X-I-T-O: Su Estrategia de Marketing Digital en 5 Pasos* (*Your Digital Marketing Strategy in 5 Steps*). Instead of taking time off to write his second book, Joe juggled writing and consulting together. By working while writing, Joe was able to leverage his clients' issues as case studies. Their real-world examples provided readers with practical and useful advice for professionals, including potential future clients.

Impact: In December 2013, after freelancing for two years, Joe incorporated his own company, Latino Link Advisors, a digital marketing strategy firm for the U.S. Hispanic market, Mexico, and Latin America. While Joe had originally intended to find a new job, he realized that in the long term it made sense to build his own company and personal brand versus starting a new job and risking getting laid off yet again.

PRACTICE OF PAUSE ADVICE

Take inventory and be grateful.
Change your mindset toward actively practicing gratitude for the many things you do and have. You will likely find yourself more content as new opportunities come your way. Schedule time to reflect and journal about your goals and accomplishments.

Take a *real* pause.
Stop running around the addictive, familiar hamster wheel. Instead, take a break, meditate, practice yoga, play golf, daydream, reconnect with friends and family, or try something new. Now is your chance. Reflect on the past, present, and future. Joe found meditation allowed him time to notice his inner conversations, rationalizations, dreams and desires, and inner demons, and it provided him with an opportunity to come to peace with them.

Create a pause journal.
A pause gives us time to reflect. What positions, responsibilities, and people did you enjoy (or not) in your previous role? Why? Use your journal to reflect on the busy times and then tap into what motivates you. Check out Passion Planner.com for a fantastic calendar and journal tool to help you plan your goals and dreams. In the words of its creator, "Passion Planner helps people break down their long- and short-term goals into more actionable steps and gives them a place to incorporate these steps into their daily lives."

Direct your passion toward social good.
What are you passionate about? What problems need to be solved in your community? Who is underserved? What yearning could you fulfill by helping them? If you are passionate about animals could you volunteer at a local animal shelter to connect and make a difference? If you want to have more impact in your community could you volunteer as a Big Brother or Big Sister? Explore a few ideas and pick one that works for you. Make a plan and take action.

Identify key relationships and allies.
During life's difficult moments, we discover, or rediscover, our true friends. Who is there for you? Whom do you trust? These people can be a sounding board and provide you with essential perspective during life's transitions. Perhaps they can introduce you to potential employers or clients. Or they can simply listen and help you explore which routes to pursue.

Find a mentor.
Would you find the perspective of an older and/or wiser

professional helpful? Think about who can help you look around corners and consider what to do next. Your mentor could be a previous boss, a family member, or a member of your professional organization. Remember that a mentorship isn't all one-sided. You need to add value and show your appreciation. Mentors can help you chart a course for something completely new, like starting a company or shifting careers.

Join a mastermind group.
A mastermind group is not a class, group coaching, or a networking group. Instead, it provides a platform for brainstorming around common goals as well as accountability and support among the group members. In addition to offering mentorship, mastermind groups can impart necessary insights about how to start up a business. Napoleon Hill introduced the concept of mastermind groups in his book *Think and Grow Rich*, and he describes them as "the coordination of knowledge and effort of two or more people, who work toward a definite purpose, in the spirit of harmony." Your team may include fellow job seekers or authors-to-be. By sharing know-how and tools, you will help one another grow and learn faster.

Design your pause around your passion.
What do you love to do but routinely think, "Oh, I don't have time for that?" Use a pause to pursue it. You may end up discovering a new passion that takes your life on a whole new career path, introduces you to a new circle of friends, or simply evolves into a new hobby.

Steve Jobs, the founder and former CEO of Apple, summed up his experience of getting laid off with a positive spin: "I didn't see it then, but it turned out that getting fired from Apple was the best thing that could have ever happened to me. The heaviness of being successful was replaced by the lightness of being a beginner again, less sure about everything. It freed me to enter one of the most creative periods of my life."[1]

The New Career Transition Pause

Before your next job begins, I recommend building in time for a few weeks to pause if at all possible. However, not everyone has that luxury. What if you need to pause now, despite future job prospects? Ask for what you want, such as an additional few days or a week (or weeks) before you start. Be firm and plan in advance what could work for you. If your new employer really wants you, a few days, or even a week, ideally, won't be difficult. If that's impossible, negotiate up front for more vacation days. Taking this time creates the space to consciously set your intention for how you want to be when you begin your next adventure, and recharge your batteries.

Make Transitions Work for You

How important is it to transition from one thing to the next, fluidly and effortlessly? Imagine you are moving from one meeting, class, or activity to the next, with a brief amount of time to spare in between. You want to be mentally and emotionally prepared when you get there. Do you expect to be ready immediately, without time to settle in? Naturally, you need time to transition.

Consider the time between jobs as an opportunity to transition. We go through countless transitions every day: getting from point A to point B, transitioning from work to a meal, or going from waking up to brushing your teeth.

How can you make a transition work for you? Raise your awareness of what's going on around you. Notice how you feel. Be mindful of your state of mind. Incorporate the familiar to help ease any transition. Set boundaries on how you spend your time. This includes reaching out to a trusted friend and sharing how you feel. Add in rituals that help structure your time and that you enjoy. Become intentional in your behavior, your expression, and how you show up. All of this will lead to a smoother transition.

Transitions can go one of two ways. They can be well planned, so things can go smoothly and as easily as possible. Or they can be erratic and rushed, with a general lack of awareness and consciousness. If things go well, a transition, or pausing, allows you time to move, reflect, and prepare for your next destination.

The Going Back to School Pause

Learning something new is a great way to pause. Many people decide to return to school—to finish a degree, learn a new discipline, or study on a part-time basis. If this is something you choose to do, it means your mind is in a state of *shoshin*, or what Zen Buddhism calls "beginner's mind." You are intuitively open to new ideas, concepts, and points of view that can help you see things differently. All you need is a little curiosity and your growth mindset.

It takes a little consciousness and planning, but with a little effort you can craft your pause while going back to school. Going back to school creates an opportunity to look at life from a new perspective, similar to a parental or family leave or a technology-free pause. You can build in a daily pause, before class once a week, or after every class.

Do you want to return to school and have a hunch some particular class would be of interest, like learning a new language or how to make pottery? You can choose a class, program, or school where you make a choice to have a growth mindset. Maybe it is in a neighboring town or even a different part of the world. It may bring you delight or struggle. Enrolling in a course that is of interest can help you align with who you are and feed your yearnings to learn, connect, or make a difference.

The Pause Without Leaving

Don't worry if you don't have the time, money, or other resources for a pause that requires you to vacation. A pause is possible anytime you choose. The best way to do this is to simply create a pause by extracting yourself from your everyday environment. Take a class or learn a new skill, as discussed. Start a new exercise routine. Host a friend for an overdue visit, or prepare a nourishing dinner party. All of these can be viewed as pauses. Remember, a pause is any intentional change in your routine where you introduce something new that makes you think or do whatever it is differently. The time that you set aside for yourself *is* the pause.

The Downshift Pause

Author David Allen, in his bestselling book *Getting Things Done*, says, "Your ability to generate power is directly proportional to your ability to relax."[2] Think about when you are at your best. You aren't in a frenetic, agitated state. You may be excited, but the sweet spot is when you are clear, relaxed, and focused. Allen tells us that this relaxed yet alert state is the secret to maximizing performance. I view pausing as an opportunity to facilitate this state to slow down, shift your behavior, or alter your environment to become more relaxed. I call this "the downshift pause." Allen shares the "mind like water" analogy, where the "perfect readiness" state in karate is when the mind takes on the same characteristics as a calm body of water. Pausing helps create this state.

Slowing down to focus *becomes* the pause. You are downshifting, and regulating your mental, physiological, and emotional states to calm and clear your mind. Focusing becomes easier. The downshift pause allows you to reach this "frictionless state" that doesn't require anything other than a conscious effort to be more relaxed and focused.

The same is true in sport. A man after my own heart, Allen

goes on to reference world-class rower Craig Lambert and how he feels when he reaches this "frictionless state" while rowing. In his book *Mind Over Water*, Lambert eloquently describes this frictionless state as "swing": "Recall the pure joy of riding on a backyard swing: an easy cycle of motion, the momentum coming from the swing itself. The swing carries us; we do not force it. We pump our legs to drive our arc higher, but gravity does most of the work. We are not so much swinging as being swung. The boat swings you."[3]

When you slow down your pace, your thoughts, your rhythm, you are changing how you move in the boat; you are downshifting. The same holds true in real life. When you relax and focus while in the midst of doing other things, this has the same effect. Are you running an errand? Take a minute and focus on your breath. Are you working on a presentation? Take a five-minute "downshift pause" to get up, move around, and do something that brings you joy or helps you meet a yearning. The key is to make a conscious choice to pause while in the midst of doing something else. Whatever it is, you can be in the midst of the activity and still establish a sense of calm.

The Physical Movement Pause

As we know, pausing can literally be any change in behavior. One way to do this is through physical movement and expression, which also helps us to feel more present and aware. Dancing and fitness classes offer a great way to pause. In my case, I wanted to be more connected to my feminine self. I was curious about a women's dance class I had heard a buzz about from a few female friends. It was called S Factor, founded by Sheila Kelley (https://sfactor.com). After a fun and inspiring teaser intro class, I signed up for six more weeks of the level-one class. Over the next month and a half, I spent my Saturday mornings learning how to express my feminine side through movement and dance. I was waking up my feminine power and getting in touch with my own sensuality, body, and movement. I think of this class as yet another pause—it was time I dedicated to learning more about my feminine qualities, getting more in touch with myself, and understanding how to leverage my feminine gifts. Any form of dance, body movement, or fitness class can become your customized pause laboratory.

Practice of Pause Moments:
Chapter 9

What type of pause resonates with you from this chapter?

Picture yourself six months after your pause. How would life be different during and after your pause? Who can you share your plan with and by when?

What would be your "pause payment," or benefits, for your time off? (Examples include peace of mind, pursuing a passion, nourishing your spirit, following a passion or dream as a result of your yearnings.)

What creative ways can you pause without leaving your job?

What is the next tangible action you need to take toward taking a pause?

Chapter 10

Tips for a Meaningful Pause

What lies behind us and what lies before us
are tiny matters compared to what lies within us.

—HENRY S. HASKINS

WHAT YOU GET out of something is a direct result of what you put into it. Here's my "best of" list for what worked and what didn't when taking a pause, regardless of duration or resources. You can take these insights and apply them to your own situation.

Create Your Ground Rules

We feel better, experience less stress, and are more comfortable when we have structure in our lives. Rules are a great way to add this. Going rule free can wreak havoc because it can be so unstructured. Pausing is an opportunity to update or remove any rules that govern how you spend your time.

Design Three to Five Rules for Your Pause

My rules centered on keeping a daily routine of a few key actions. I credit my fellow pauser and intervention friend, Kathleen, for introducing this concept. Her advice to leave the house by 10:00 a.m. daily "or else you'll go insane" stuck with me. When I didn't want to change my rules after my first week, I knew they were good:

1. Make my bed when I get up.
2. Leave the house by 10:00 a.m.
3. Shower once a day (I actually needed this rule to prevent my own laziness).
4. Spend a maximum of thirty minutes at a time online (e-mails, Web sites, social media).
5. Spend an hour of the day outside the house learning an activity of my choice.

My first two weeks were a transition from my old routine into a new one. Having rules and structure helped me feel organized. I spent my mornings in a café, laptop in hand and egg burrito on the table. I settled into a routine. I continued to mix things up a bit so it didn't feel too structured. I strolled through Chinatown or went to a nearby museum. Other days I saw a matinee. Having rules helped me motivate, follow my intentions, learn my strengths, tune in to what I wanted to do, and relax.

Incorporate Self-Care and Nourishing Pause Practices

Rules are helpful—but what about ways to care for your emotional well-being? This is where self-care techniques like those listed below come in handy.[1] I recommend trying each of them and seeing what sticks.

- **Wrap up in a warm, cozy blanket during your downtime.** You can do this by yourself or with a friend or partner. Imagine it is your own adult-swaddle blanket, and as you wrap yourself up, embody feeling secure and safe.
- **Gently rock back and forth.** Just like when we were babies, rocking has an enormous soothing quality about it. You can be in a blanket while you rock or without it. A rocking chair or swing is ideal, but if you don't have that, sit on the floor in whatever way is comfortable and rock gently from side to side.
- **Adopt a stuffed animal.** Your "stuffie" will love you unconditionally, and you can always practice being gentle and kind with your stuffie, which is good practice for doing the same thing for yourself. If you think I'm crazy, try it. (I may still be crazy.) I carried my stuffed monkey, Ellie, around for an entire month as I learned to care for her. She even went on dates! Years later, Ellie continues to hang out with me and comes with me on trips. Why is this recommended? Imagine your stuffed animal as an extension of you! He or she is your inner child. When he or she becomes visible, you can begin to notice how you care for yourself, as you care for your stuffed animal. I'm

not saying you have to take her on dates, but having a stuffed animal is an easy way to practice self-care.

■ **Take a five-minute nourishment pause.** Make your favorite tea or coffee. Have a one-song dance party in your living room. Buy yourself a beautiful plant or flowers and tell it how much you appreciate it. Call a friend to connect. Ask for or give a hug. Do anything that makes you feel nourished.

Make a "What Nourishes Me" and "Say Adieu" List

What activities make you feel happy from the inside out? What do you enjoy that makes your soul come alive? Here are mine:

What Nourishes Me

■ Taking a 3:00 p.m. herbal or iced tea break
■ Having a few friends over for a meal once a month
■ Sharing what's going on in my life with friends who support me
■ Watching a good movie after cooking a healthy and tasty meal
■ Exercising and feeling good in my body: hiking, biking, yoga, dancing, or moving in some way
■ Writing: journaling or blogging when I want to share or reflect

Make sure what is on this list gets incorporated into your pause. If you have limited time, select your top one or two.

Next list the habits to say adieu to, ones that make you feel constricted, drained, or unhappy. Here are mine:

Say Adieu

- Biting my nails
- Bingeing on anything: TV, eating, drinking, shopping . . .
- Checking e-mails or social media for more than one hour a day

What would your lists look like? Write them down and periodically check in. By creating these lists, you are incorporating nourishing habits into your pause and raising your awareness for what is important (and what you want to avoid) as you maximize your time.

Establish Accountability

Old habits die hard. Establishing accountability can help you change your behavior over time. One effective way to do this is to use "implementation intentions."[2] These are statements to keep yourself in check as you implement new thoughts and behaviors, which ideally become habits over time. They aren't mean to be punishments; rather, they are ways you can hold yourself accountable.

As Drs. Bob and Judith Wright point out, "Studies show that when you use the if-then format to spell out in advance what you're going to do when or under what circumstances, you are much more likely to put your intention into action."[3] Conversely, if you break a rule, you can create a consequence for not following through. Don't think of them as punishments. They help keep us conscious of how we want to behave and act in life and reinforce new ways of thinking or being. They are a way to implement the changes you want to make and keep yourself accountable. You'll know they are effective if you end up shifting your behavior and breaking old habits.

Here are a few of the implementation intention statements that help me stay on track:

- If I don't make my bed before work, then I do ten push-ups before bedtime.
- If (and when) I wake up, then I pray and meditate before I leave the house.
- If I go out to dinner, then I choose the healthiest menu option.
- If I notice a yearning to connect, then I will express it and fulfill it (make eye contact or phone a friend).

Tell someone about your lists and if-then statements as another way to be accountable.

Find Your Alignment

Pausing isn't an excuse to clean out the garage or finish that half-written novel. It's not about going through the motions. As part of this focus on the inner self, some of the most rewarding pausing is gaining introspection into what you truly want. If you take this time and see what's out of alignment, you'll be able to discover how to get more alignment into your life.

When I took time off from Google, I needed to figure out where I was out of alignment. It wasn't until I sat down with Margaret's boss, Bill, that he matter-of-factly told me, "Rachael, your skill set isn't a match for this role. I know Margaret has the best intentions for you, and you need to find a job that works best for what you're good at." In two short sentences, Bill summarized my mental battle that was so obvious to others, but had been my blind spot. If I had looked at this conversation under a magnifying lens, I would see my situation wasn't about me "underperforming," which was what I'd heard Margaret tell me time and time again. I considered that maybe my performance review wasn't really about my *performance*, but about my *alignment*. What Margaret was saying was that "my strengths weren't a fit," without telling me as straight-up as Bob did. Margaret was simply giving me the opportunity to take a job that aligned with my strengths.

How often do we have the courage to change or seek a situation that's 100 percent aligned with what we want or need? If we're not in alignment, chances are we've compromised part of ourselves to please someone else or "do the right thing." We're taught from an early age that it's okay to compromise. However, this belief is faulty, and it leads to a tendency to disrespect ourselves.

When we are aligned, it's because we are motivated by our purpose. If we don't know what that is, it can be difficult to know what path or situation works best. Anyone can ask on a daily basis, "How aligned do I feel today, or in a certain situation, or even in a relationship with this person?" You quickly realize what is and isn't working in your best interest. You can also reflect on whether your own core values—the principles you operate from—are congruent with your situation.

The most useful advice I received while trying to examine

my inner self was from a career coach at Google named Becky. She recommended I take a day to go to a remote, deserted beach, sit in the sand dunes, and write down what I wanted to do at the end of my pause.

She was onto something. How often might you come up with a solution to a dilemma if you allowed yourself time to reflect? It likely doesn't require perching in sand dunes, but anytime you can minimize external distractions and deeply listen, ideas may bubble up that you didn't even know existed. Instead of planning trips, or busifying life, ask yourself at least once a week, "What am I aligned with?" Something new may emerge from this openness and lead to more ideas. By following Becky's advice, I figured out purpose for my pause and a way to focus on my inner self.

PAUSE STORY
Lissa Rankin, MD

From Overworked Ob-Gyn to Holistic Health Visionary and Bestselling Author

In 2006, Lissa was working full time as an ob-gyn in Southern California, but she felt unfulfilled. She had become disillusioned with the health care system and realized she no longer wanted to continue being overworked and out of integrity.

Budget: Lissa sold her home and liquidated retirement funds to help cover expenses, which included covering medical malpractice insurance (cost for that alone was $120,000) and more than two years of living expenses for herself and her family. She found herself in serious debt, which took several years to reverse.

Duration: Two years

Goal: No set goal, other than to figure out next steps

Trigger: Lissa was already on multiple medications to maintain her sanity when she underwent what she calls her perfect storm. Within a two-week span, several major life events happened at once: Lissa gave birth, by C-section, to her daughter; her dog died; her healthy young brother wound up with full-blown liver failure as a rare side effect of a common antibiotic; and her father passed away. This series of events was the last straw. Lissa felt as if she were on a freight train that had hit a wall and gone off the rails. She was left putting the pieces back together, one at a time, and found herself needing the time to do so.

Looking back, Lissa would diagnose herself with what shamans would call "soul loss," where a reconnection with her soul needed to happen to regain meaning, direction, vitality, mission, purpose, identity, and genuine connection. She had lost touch with her inner voice.

Plan: It took Lissa a full year to extricate herself completely from her medical practice. It felt like an act of rebellion. After all, doctors just don't take pauses, let alone an extended one. She wasn't even allowed to take more than a monthlong postpartum leave, even though she was an ob-gyn and had just had a C-section. Lissa knew she had to devise a plan to avoid falling off the deep end. She quit her job, sold her house in San Diego, and moved her family to Monterey, California. Even as a medical professional, there were still plenty of expenses to figure out, including malpractice insurance for another two years and expenses for a new baby. As a result, the bills piled up, but Lissa stayed firm. She knew she couldn't return to the lifestyle that no longer was working for her. She spent two years healing, writing, painting, and hiking.

Impact: Lissa had lost her sense of purpose. She had forgotten who she was. After two years of what she calls "waiting and becoming," she finally realized which path she was meant to walk. Prior to her pause, Lissa thought her life as a healer and in medicine was over. Medicine had broken her heart, and she wanted to stop forever. But she realized that even if you quit your job, you can't quit your calling. She just had to find a new way to interface with it.

Lissa reconnected with her spiritual side. She spent a lot of time listening to her inner voice, which she fondly calls her "Inner Pilot Light." Her path was guided. Signs from the universe appeared everywhere. Her soul awakened. The rest, as she says, is history.

Today, Lissa lives in Marin County where the land meets the sea—literally. Her house overlooks the Pacific Ocean and every day she is surrounded by the beauty of life. Quoting from her Web site, she is "a *New York Times* bestselling author; her books include *Mind Over Medicine, The Fear Cure*, and *The Anatomy of a Calling*. She is a physician, a speaker, and founder of the Whole Health Medicine Institute. She is on a mission to merge science and spirituality in a way that not only facilitates the health of the individual but also uplifts the health of the collective. Bridging seemingly disparate worlds, Lissa is a connector, collaborator, curator, and amplifier, broadcasting both her unique visionary ideas and also those of cutting-edge visionaries she trusts, especially in the field of her latest research into what she calls 'Sacred Medicine.'"[4]

PRACTICE OF PAUSE ADVICE

Pausing helps the right answer appear.
Many of us tend to get so busy forcing our way through life. Now Lissa realizes that when she's confused, unclear about a decision, or otherwise feeling befuddled, the solution is not to try harder or think more. It's to get away and do less. It is only then that the answers show up. Not just any answer, but the right answer.

Know your pause is temporary.
Once you realize a pause is not indefinite, a lot of anxiety disappears. Give yourself permission to relax, and try not to rush right into the next thing. Enjoy your time. Cook fresh meals from farmers' market produce, or do things in town. It is the "space between stories" that normalizes our experiences, as author Charles Eisenstein says.[5] The more you normalize, the more you see we all have times in our lives when we find ourselves "in between."

Follow the bread crumbs.
If you are brave enough to find a bread crumb that leads you to pause, follow the next bread crumb. Most of our journeys do not follow a linear-type business plan.

Be patient for guidance.
It's divine timing, not yours. You are valuable and worthy and perfect, wherever you are on your hero's journey. Trust that and continue to follow the bread crumbs. Eventually you will end up somewhere greater than you ever envisioned.

Take the Pause Purpose Pledge

Purpose is the why of our life; it is what matters to you and allows you to create a life that's meaningful to you, moment by moment.[6] Pausing gives you the space to discover meaning in the moment. It is an opportunity to enjoy the discovery of who you are becoming as you make room for something new to emerge. Even if you have never thought about your purpose (and many of us don't), discovering what matters to you is a way you can connect with yourself and get inspired. Your Pause Purpose Pledge reflects that. This pledge is a fluid statement, which you can update at any time to reflect your commitment and why pausing is important to you. Join the Pause Purpose Pledge community at www.rachaelomeara.com and share your pledge. I recommend reading your Pause Purpose Pledge once a day for thirty days. It can serve as an empowering reminder about your commitment to yourself and help you integrate it into your postpause lifestyle.

PAUSE PURPOSE PLEDGE

I, [your name here], commit to pause and intentionally shift my behavior. I trust I am in the right place. I choose to learn from this experience and apply it in a way that gives more meaning to my life. As of [today's date], one action I will take toward my pause purpose is and why it matters is:

———————————————————————

This pledge goes into effect immediately.

[your signature]

After my pause I realized my purpose is to be an agent of change. No matter what I do on a given day or why I'm doing it, I aim to change myself and others for the better. I yearn to connect with others, feel alive, and make a difference. I can teach something new to a coworker, inspire someone to do something differently, or help someone realize that taking a pause and shifting an area of life is okay. It doesn't mean everything I do results in change, but I am always acting out of my sense of purpose to be an agent of change for myself and others.

Celebrate Yourself!

Once you take the Pause Purpose Pledge, celebrate! You've taken a very important step to creating a meaningful pause. Practice a nourishing or self-care behavior, such as those covered earlier. Will you go for a walk outside? Listen to a favorite song and have a dance party? Take a few minutes today, recognize your wins, and celebrate.

Identify Your Strengths

Think about it yourself, but also ask others what they think are your strengths. Note the patterns or themes that emerge, and write down what you are hearing and learning.

I've mentioned Tom Rath's *StrengthsFinder 2.0.* It's a great resource and provides a thorough self-assessment to identify your core strengths. Using the book and the accompanying Web site, you will receive a detailed report of your top strengths, and recommendations for career choices based on your input.[7]

These were my top five themes (listed in order of strongest attribute):

- Achiever
- Positivity
- Woo (as in "wooing" someone)
- Learner
- Competition

Based on my informal questions to friends and my *Strengths-Finder 2.0* results, I had a good handle on what skills and roles I wanted to pursue. Some of them resonated with me (I love "wooing the crowd"), but others were not as obvious. Both helped me learn more about myself in an objective, practical way.

Communicating Strengths

While on my pause, I started talking about my strengths when asked and how I'd apply them in my next role. I was allowing my inner voice to emerge and be heard. I felt secure sharing my truth. Maintaining eye contact and admitting my uncertainty and fears were refreshing and new to me. I wasn't very good at it before pausing. When I became vulnerable, I was giving others permission, whether they realized it or not, to match my vulnerability. It was an important lesson I learned every time I had a conversation.

When you are accessible in this way, you signal that it's okay for others to do the same. It feels affirming because you are allowing your honest, authentic self a moment to emerge. You create the opportunity for others to see the real you. When this happens, every interaction becomes an act—a gift—of self-care. You meet your yearnings to be seen and heard. You are with yourself at a deeper level and, as a result, you are inviting others in to meet you there. When I was asked what I would do next, instead of glossing over this issue and giving a generic answer, I shared my real truths.

"Well, I thought a lot about my strengths the last three months and how I could incorporate them into what to do next. At Google, there's so much opportunity. I realized my strengths were working with people and building relationships and relating well with others. I'm an experienced industry veteran in online advertising, and I'm pretty good at explaining technical concepts to different groups of people."

How would you honestly answer that question? Even if you don't know, stating that is being vulnerable.

"It occurred to me that these skills relate well to working with clients. I'd love a job where I can leverage my experience or technical expertise from past roles."

As long as you speak what you honestly feel, your listener will likely show genuine interest, locking eyes and giving you his or her undivided attention. You are a breath of fresh air. Speaking honestly and authentically is rare. People know it when they hear or see it. Think about the last time someone was vulnerable with you: even if you were uncomfortable, it was no ordinary conversation. Even if you freak someone else out because they aren't ready or prepared to meet you at that level, give yourself some credit. You are honoring your authentic self and how you feel in the moment by saying what matters and what comes to you. Your job is to take care of yourself, and not worry about how anyone else reacts to you. That is honorable, and it's real self-respect.

Think of Your Pause as an Experiment

Think of your time off as an experiment—an opportunity for enrichment and lively adventure. The key is, once again, maintaining a growth mindset. If you do this, everything becomes an opportunity.

I conducted a few experiments during my pause. One was to be more Zen-like or calm. I thought yoga could help with that. My first mini trip, to Austin, Texas, introduced me to Bikram yoga, which is performed in a mere 102-degree environment. I was afraid I'd overheat, hate it, pass out, or suffer my way through. To my surprise, I liked it. When I returned to San Francisco, knowing that it would improve my flexibility, I created the intention to attend two classes per week.

Another experiment was to try being a part-time bike tour guide. After looking at my strengths, I realized I was passionate about biking and showing others around by bike. I applied for and got a part-time position, on weekends, as a wine country tour guide. This experiment gave me one of the most fun and rewarding jobs I'd had in some time—all in wine country!

These experiments aligned with my yearnings, values, and passions. I yearned to feel alive and have fun. I valued meeting new people, physical activity, and sharing my passions for biking and hosting. I chose these activities because they aligned with my heart and core values of health, spending time outside, and meeting and getting to know others who had mutual interests. As a result, I felt fulfilled and happy.

Act on experiments you may have passed up before your pause, but that are driven by deeper yearnings, passions, and values. Let your inner guide lead you to find out what those experiments may be.

Just Say Yes

One of the golden rules of improv actors is to always say yes. It's one way to stay open to opportunities, no matter what. Embrace your growth mindset, and say yes to as much as possible, especially to new things. If you catch yourself saying "not today" or "that's not what I do," practice the art of mental flossing and TASERing your thoughts. Realize that your brain is up to its old tricks that have worked so well to keep from changing for your own good. The more you say yes to larger risks or opportunities, the more you are retraining your brain.

Saying yes is one more secret to a successful pause. You can expand new frontiers, explore new territory, and get out of your comfort zone. Look for opportunities to say yes where you may have said no in the past. Invitations to new activities or interests that you've always wanted to pursue may appear. Here are some ways you can say yes, whether it's an incremental step or a leap into the unknown.

- Pick one day a week where you say yes to anything you are asked (keep it legal, please).
- Say yes to an activity you have always thought about but haven't yet pursued. Make a plan to do it on your pause.
- Take an improv class. Find an improv theater in your area. Intro classes range from a single workshop to several months.

■ Play the improv-based "yes, and" game. Here's how it works: Say "yes, and" to any idea that's proposed, then build and develop it into something else. The opposite—saying "yes, but" or "no"—limits growth and cuts the idea short of its potential. As an example, let's say your friend asks you if you want to go to lunch. You can reply, "Yes, and let's make sure we eat ice cream, too." You can clue your friend in to respond in a "yes, and" format after your response, too, to keep the game going. Next time you catch yourself wanting to say no in conversation or to yourself, say "yes, and" along with your next thought. Play this game with a friend and see what happens.

Expand Your Comfort Zone

This diagram sums up this concept nicely. I was inspired by some art I came across in social media. It is a powerful reminder that we must leave our comfort zone in order to find the magic in our lives.

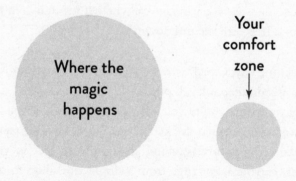

Our limbic brains like the familiar and safe, but not very magically inclined, comfort zone. We don't have any looming threats to worry about. When we leave our comfort zone, there's associated risk and discomfort while our brains learn and rewire for new experiences.

A pause is an ideal time to do, think, and be different as you leave your comfort zone. That's why pauses can be so magical. Outside our comfort zone is where we flourish: it's also where we maximize our capacity for learning and growth. We feel alive and present as we take on new experiences and carve new neural networks. Expect to feel afraid or anxious. Remember to TASER your limiting beliefs, name your yearnings, and go for meeting your yearnings on your pause. You are in new, magical, uncharted territory.

Pick one thing that is out of your comfort zone and go for it. Use your growth mindset. When you take small, incremental steps over and over again, your comfort zone expands. If you have enough of these experiences, eventually you begin to think differently. Expect to feel uncomfortable. It is a good sign that you are learning and growing! When this happens, you start living in new ways that were once unimaginable. You find the magic.

Outside My Comfort Zone

A friend of mine, Liz, invited me to join her one night for a salsa lesson. I realized how much I liked to move around a dance floor. Here I was at salsa, submerged within the Latin beat, clueless how to coordinate my feet, but I felt good and was in tune with my body. I stuck with it, knowing I had a lot more to learn, and had fun.

Even though I felt uncomfortable and self-conscious at

first, I danced through my fear of salsa and took it on as a challenge to learn a new, fun skill. I bought a set of group lessons. I became more comfortable about my dancing and less self-conscious. I surprised myself when I started looking forward to Monday nights. Before I knew it, I had expanded my own comfort zone and started to enjoy salsa. This led to new friends, dates, and experiences and is a great reminder of why it's important to go beyond our comfort zone to "find the magic" and live fully in our lives.

Stay Present

Just as we program ourselves to stay in our comfort zone, we have the same tendency when we think about the future. It's easy to get caught up in the what-ifs and start feeling anxious. When we focus on the future, we are no longer in the present moment. That moment becomes lost.

A few examples:

- Making predictions or anticipating a future event or outcome as a result of a present action or decision ("If I do X now, that means Y will happen later, and I'll feel happy/sad/fearful/etc., and such and such won't happen," etc.).
- Allowing your concerns about the future to stall you in the present ("When will I get married? When will I make more money? When am I going to get promoted? I can't wait until I lose ten pounds so I can . . ."). If you're present, there's nothing to worry about.

Gabrielle Bernstein, as mentioned earlier in chapter 6, influenced my awareness to stay present. She coined a term that hit home for me: "future tripping."[8] Instead of being in the present moment, you are worrying about what you can or can't do sometime in the future. If we related this to taking a pause to shift careers, an example of future tripping would be "How will I ever find another job after my pause?" You are in your head instead of being in the here and now. You're off somewhere else, frantic about what will happen later.

Future tripping tends to produce worrying, which can increase levels of cortisol, the body's stress hormone. This can perpetuate more thoughts about fictional scenarios. This is not ideal for staying grounded, present, or focused, all of which are likely proving elusive to you and why you are pausing in the first place.

If you find yourself future tripping, here are a few ways to bring yourself back to the here and now.[9]

- Ask yourself, "What am I not noticing, right now?" Notice what you're feeling.
- Ask yourself, "What is this moment presenting to me, right now?"
- Call yourself out. Say out loud, "There I go again, future tripping." Then turn toward your surroundings and take in your environment using your sensory perception. One of the quickest ways to become more present and be in your body is to notice your emotions and the sensory-grounded data of what you experience through your five senses.

Journal to Stay Present

As I've stated already, each journal entry is an opportunity to be a little more present. If you're a creative type, buy a sketchbook, a writing journal, or a combination of both. Create a personal journal, a blog, or a vlog (video blog) about your pause. Describe each day. What did you do? How did it make you feel? Were you excited, nervous, hungry? Detail the simplest of tasks, like making a delicious dinner, going for a bike ride, or walking in the park. Each is a story to share. Writing down even the most mundane thoughts or ideas is a way to focus on your inner self and capture a stream of thought that you may not even realize you had. Start with the questions in the Practice of Pause Moments in this book. I recommend starting your own individual pause journal, or pausebook, to stay present and maximize what you learn and discover about yourself during this transformative time.

Take a Solo Vacation—Whether at Home or Away

Taking time off is a luxury. It may not be an option to leave a job for one reason or another, no matter how much you may want or need the break. So what can you do instead? How can you continue to do what you do (work, care for someone else, be a parent) *and* take a pause?

The answer is easier than you think. Start incorporating actions into your life that will allow you to incorporate intentional shifts in what you do. You set the duration. Here are a few examples:

- **Taking a digital pause.** As discussed earlier, even if you don't make this your main type of pause, it's still worth trying out as an experiment for a day or longer.
- **Taking a renewed purpose pause.** For a specific period

of time, take action on an idea or project that you have been meaning to start for some time.

- **Taking a change of life pause.** Embark on a healthier lifestyle for a week (e.g., cut out fried foods) or start a new exercise regimen (e.g., walking or jogging once a week).
- **Taking a change of heart pause.** Dedicate one or two days to a new initiative. Spend that time figuring out how you want your world to shift.
- **Taking a change of intent pause.** Set your intention each day to focus on what makes you happy.

Don't dismiss the idea of taking a pause if it's not ideal timing—you can incorporate many of these concepts, or sub-concepts, into your daily life by dedicating your next week off to pausing. The point is to take action to shift how you currently live your life. You can completely remove yourself from your existing world or take one step toward doing something that makes you happier and more satisfied or brings more meaning to your life.

If you do actually have the time and resources to travel somewhere by yourself, do it! Plan a solo trip. Doing it annually can be a good way to take a time-out to reflect on your life, milestones, and personal growth. It can be a weekend, a day, or whatever length works. I know it can be daunting to indulge yourself in personal time away from your existing world. It can be uncomfortable to visit a beautiful place all by yourself. Part of the magic of going solo is to discover an experience that you create for yourself. Go where you want, when you want, and on your terms. Think of it like another act of self-care to focus on your inner self. Even if it's for twenty-four hours, it is another experiment and opportunity to find the magic outside of your comfort zone. After all, aren't we always supposed to be with other people? That's what's expected, but by no means is it the way it has to be. By taking alone time, you are committing yourself to all the things I've already stated above. It works. Having no one to prioritize but yourself provides a new way to focus on what matters most to you.

PAUSE STORY
Steve Sisgold

From Burned-Out Sales Executive to Living His Purpose

Steve was making great money in his corporate sales job at a large business equipment firm. He'd had a knack for reading people ever since he was a kid, and it served him well in sales. Not only was he killing it in his role, he was outselling all the other salespeople and was ranked the number one salesperson, out of five hundred people, for several years. However, over a few sales cycles, he noticed that the more he sold, the more his company wanted to reduce his commission checks. There was opposition brewing at the corporate headquarters, and something needed to change.

Budget: A few thousand dollars in savings

Duration: Two months

Goal: Reinvigorate his mind, body, and soul and listen to his inner voice

Trigger: Steve had the opportunity to ask what was happening in a meeting with a vice president of the company. He was told that there were changes to policies and that, more or less, this was how things were going to be. He was offered an opportunity to move across the country to the home office in New England. The offer hinged on serious caveats, and Steve squirmed at the thought. Steve left the meeting frustrated and confused.

When he returned to his routine after that meeting, he found he wasn't growing; he was waning and getting by. He wasn't excited to get up in the morning, like he once was, and do his core job. Instead, he found himself drawn to other interests that stemmed from his creative side. He wanted to feed his musical talents and spend more time playing the guitar and singing. He had a desire to teach people things, and to write more about his own personal experiences in sales and what he'd learned from reading people along the way.

Enough was enough. Steve quit his sales job and decided to focus on his creative passions, even if it was for a short time span. He had no idea how long he would take off, but he knew he needed to do something creative, even if it was only for one week.

Plan: Steve decided to pack a bag, get in the car, and drive. He wanted to go somewhere, anywhere, and just sit for one week. He made a loose plan to drive down south from San Francisco and see where he wound up. When he got to Los Angeles, he decided he wanted to go to a retreat, so he looked in the phone book and found a hot spring complex outside of San Diego. He knew hot springs and quiet would help him get answers.

And was he right. At the hot springs he was able to relax and allow his thoughts to drift. He paid attention to his inner voice for clues about what his next steps might be. This quiet allowed other thoughts to emerge that he hadn't heard before.

Ideas started to pop up. He asked himself, "What can I do next that matters?" He spent the rest of the week reflecting. He noticed his best ideas came to him without any effort when he went swimming in the pools. He wrote them down. He thought about what was needed in his community, and what was missing that he could provide. He started to get visuals of helping other people connect. His inner voice kept telling him the same thing. He was here to help others follow their dreams. He was here to connect people.

Within a week of being on his quiet retreat and soaking in the waters, Steve came up with his idea: create a business around networking and social events for the local Bay Area community. He called it the Marin Business Exchange. Nothing like it existed in the area. It was the pre-Internet era, and social networking required going somewhere to meet new people and say hello in person. Steve knew he was the right man for the job.

Impact: Steve returned to the Bay Area, invigorated to create his new business, dive into his marketing plan, and create his first event. He felt renewed and alive again. His body and mind felt good, and he was energized to get started.

Within the first few months of his monthly networking events, Steve amassed a following. His next opportunity began to unfold: coaching people on how to overcome their own blocks and authentically market themselves. Today, we call this personal branding. Soon he had a second income stream coming in. A third income stream evolved from support groups that formed among those wanting to pursue their dreams.

As Steve worked more with his clients, he began to notice patterns in their body language. Some people would cross their arms when they talked about their blocks. Other people would bounce their legs up and down when something specific was mentioned. His next business idea arrived: honing his practice to help others release blocks and know more about themselves using their own "body intelligence." He built yet another new business, called Whole Body Intelligence, or WBI. Over the years, he's hosted dozens of retreats in Mexico, Hawaii, New Mexico, and other beautiful, inspiring destinations.

"It's incredible to think that all of this evolved from my original pause back at Club Mud," Steve remarks fondly. "It keeps evolving: the ideas, events, clients, support groups, workshops, and now my books and consulting on body intelligence."

Today, Steve is a full-time author, coach, trainer, and speaker. He's in charge of his time, income, and future. He agrees it can be scary, stressful, and blissful at any given time. As a blogger and published author, sometimes Steve feels like he's back in college, under deadline for a term paper. He has met incredible people and traveled to wonderful places as a result of his new career path.

PRACTICE OF PAUSE ADVICE

Listen to your body.
Taking a pause can be a very spiritual experience if you see it as a growth opportunity and a chance to listen to your inner voice and physical sensations within. To learn more about how to tune in to your body, Steve offers a thirty-day program in his book. For his book, a free body awareness assessment, and more, check out www.whole bodyintelligence.com.

Make a commitment and pick an environment.

Figure out where you are going, and how long you can stay. Steve recommends picking an environment you feel safe and nurtured in and really committing to it. He asks questions like, "Do you like land or water? Do you prefer mountains or the beach? Do you thrive on weekend getaways? A park or anywhere in nature you feel safe is a great place to start, even if it's for an afternoon." He also suggests, "Ask someone to cover your responsibilities, and unplug if you can. Otherwise, you'll be forced to fall into old habits while attempting to pause. Remember, commit to what you can, but commit to *something*."

Whatever you decide, make a plan and get specific and stick to it for thirty days.

Pick a date and time and write it down so you don't forget. As we learned earlier, the physical act of writing has a neurological effect on the brain. Similar to Steve's thirty-day Whole Body Intelligence lifestyle plan, aim to do something for thirty days. Scientific research shows that it takes at least thirty days to rewire your brain. If you hop from one thing to the next, whether it's a relationship, a job, or a traumatic life event, there's no opportunity to create new neural pathways in the brain. These new pathways create larger and new neural networks that allow new ideas and habits to emerge, which means you may think and act differently, and things will shift for you.

Plan to work with teachers and coaches who do what you want to do.

Once you are aware of your body and commit to pausing, you don't have to do it on your own. Find an expert in what you want to learn. Seek out the next level of support, or find someone who already has done what you want to do. For example, if you want to get in shape, join a gym or a fitness class or hire a personal trainer. If you want to think about a new career, invest your time and money in a career coach who specializes in this area. Expect to make an investment, as many things worth your time are worth your money. Steve says, "I go to people who have done what I desire to do. I've paid a thousand dollars an hour to sit with people who were experts in their field, and to this day I use that knowledge."

Be resilient and allow ideas to evolve.
Once you allow the space to get quiet, ideas will come, and they will lead you to the next idea, and the next idea after that. Some will be great ideas that align in perfect synergy. Some may flop or be a disaster. Continue to stay on your path. If you feel overwhelmed, go to the "safe space" you committed to while pausing, whether it's nature, the beach, a hot spring, or your backyard, and recalibrate.

Practice of Pause Moments:
Chapter 10

What are a few rules to enforce for your pause and how will you keep them in place? Take the Pause Purpose Pledge at www.rachaelomeara.com and share it with at least one other person and/or the online community.

Assess your strengths by asking others who know you well what your strengths are and write them down.

What experiment would you create for your pause? What is out of your comfort zone? What can you say yes to?

Start a "present moment" journal (aka pausebook). Write only in present tense. Capture how you feel and what you see, hear, taste, feel, and smell. Avoid writing a narrative or story. Write down any other experiences or thoughts about staying present. What observations about yourself do you have on staying present?

Chapter 11

Reentry Postpause

When you make the finding yourself—even if you're the last person
on Earth to see the light—you'll never forget it.

— CARL SAGAN

YOU HAVE FOUND the initiative to pause and determined your intentions. You are in touch with your yearnings. You've decided on a plan of action (or nonaction). You have gleaned new insights from your pause, are more aware, and are choosing to live life differently as a result.

What if you could keep this going long after your pause is over?

Imagine yourself as an astronaut about to reenter Earth's orbit from deep space. Your mission is to return to where you came from safely and successfully. However, the stratosphere is often turbulent, full of potential problems for reentry. Like any astronaut, you know there is a series of maneuvers to help you travel through unscathed.

Returning from a well-intentioned pause is not much different. During the astronaut's return, the body takes on overwhelming forces: physical, mental, emotional, and even spiritual.

Similarly, your ship must undergo its own checklist to ensure it returns safely to where it came from.

What's at risk? You may get stressed out or cause yourself unnecessary suffering, worrying about what to do next. You may feel hopeless or frustrated, or some other emotional strain, as you start to think about changes or ways you want to be different. You may forget everything you learned and revert back to your old habits and ways. Anything you learn has the potential to be lost and forgotten. As much as we love the idea of change, we can easily find ourselves back in old habits. That's why reentry is a critical component of pausing.

Reentry is when you decide what to do next and how to do it. You are either in or almost back in the fold of normal, everyday life and society. Whether you've traveled for two years or escaped the clutches of technology for a day or two, you require time to transition into the world you left.

Building In Transition Time

If you took an extended pause, reentry includes reintegrating into the job force, taking on a new career path, or starting a new chapter of your life. It's an opportunity to continue your pause or growth mindset. If you never ended up physically changing your environment, you can keep the pause flames burning by integrating the feelings, thoughts, and insights you experienced.

It's important to build in time to transition as you return from a pause. Who wants to be jolted into reality without any time to adjust? Do yourself a favor and think about how much time you need to successfully and realistically transition from your pause. It could be the traveling time back to home from some period away, an hour before you turn on your digital devices, or the interval it takes to walk down the hallway before you enter a meeting. Depending on the type of pause you have, you may not need any transition time. Regardless, it's always a good idea to be aware of when you transition, so you can prepare as needed.

Takeaways, Growth, and Purpose Alignment

How can you implement key takeaways from your pause into your everyday life? It may mean maintaining a healthy lifestyle, keeping your growth mindset, practicing self-care techniques, sticking with a new habit or skill that feels nourishing, or meeting a yearning and feeling fulfilled. It can bring you closer to what matters to you, or your purpose. It's possible to bring them into your postpause world with a little thought.

Question 1: What Did You Learn?

What did you learn from pausing? What you learn is the most valuable return on investment (ROI) possible. *What* you do may not change after you return from your pause, but *how* you do it can. By identifying what you learned and then applying this to your routine, you can continue your pause mindset. If you are more present or aware after your pause, your quality of life will likely also shift.

You may discover (or rediscover) what makes you tick, your yearnings, your passions, and what you want to continue, to start, or to stop. You may learn a little or a lot in any of the seven main areas of life: your body, self, family, relationships, career, community, or spiritual side. You may tap into a deeper sense of how satisfied you are in these areas and learn what you will or will not tolerate.

One of my biggest pause takeaways was that even if I returned to the exact same role or career path, I could choose how I showed up to do my job entirely differently from the past. I learned what my strengths were and what would make me feel more fulfilled and aligned at work. I discovered my yearnings—to matter and to have more connection with others. On the tactical front, I learned I wanted to build and/or maintain relationships with clients. I also wanted to be more engaged and to use my strengths of achieving and influencing in my next role. Sales was a natural fit and became the focus role for my job search.

Let's say a key takeaway postpause is that you want to spend more time with your family or partner. Get creative for your solution, and remember to maintain your growth mindset. Whatever your takeaway is, ask yourself, "Based on what I learned, how can I do X differently so that Y occurs?" In this example, you could ask yourself, "How could I work differently so that I can enjoy more quality time at home?" Below are a few hypothetical ideas.

1. Make a plan once a week to spend uninterrupted quality time together. What could you adjust to make this happen? How can you continue it? What ground rules can you set? What activities would you do?
2. Make a plan to say hello by either calling or writing and share how you feel once a day.
3. Create a few boundaries that separate your work life from your family life. It may mean carving out set

times when you are unavailable, or getting up earlier to do something to make time for something else later.

You can come up with a few ideas for what you want to do more or less of, depending on what you learned.

Question 2: How Did You Grow?

Growth means doing things differently as a result of what you learned. Do you have a new skill or hobby? Are you more aware of your emotions or environment? Do you feel more alive, awake, and engaged?

Let's imagine your pause is taking a few minutes every morning to focus inward while you get ready for your day. Every morning, you lock eyes in the mirror, take a deep breath, and tell yourself how much you matter, or how adorable you are. (If you haven't done this, I encourage you to try it.) This is an example of doing something differently as a result of pausing. In this case, you are literally looking at yourself differently in a positive, affirming way.

Prior to my pause, I was way too attached to checking social media sites. I indulged in this soft addiction when I watched TV, felt bored, or wanted to procrastinate. I was sucked into the social media vortex where I'd blink and thirty minutes would disappear while I looked at photos of my friends, funny videos, or random, immaterial messages.

In order to grow, I needed to stay hyperaware of how I spent my time online to avoid falling into the "endless scrolling" trap. I made a rule: allow five minutes at a time for social media, with six hours between sessions. I created a second rule to not check social media until after work. I decided not to check it at all during my weeklong intentional solo vacation. Today, I'm more aware of how I spend my time on social media; my rules helped me create a system that works for me. The urge to use it is still there, but I am more aware of how I use it and am better at setting limits.

Question 3: Do You Need a New Path?

After much consideration during my pause, I decided that my company aligned with my overall purpose to be an agent of change to help others learn and grow. I knew I wanted to work at Google for the foreseeable future, but I had to find a job that fit with my strengths: managing relationships and business with clients. I decided to return to Google two months into my three-month pause. My strategy was to line up opportunities that matched my strengths. Google supported career growth and internal job transfers. I also had a backup plan: if I didn't find a role within my ninety-day time frame, I would look outside of Google for a business development sales role. I interviewed for and landed a position as an account manager on the DoubleClick Ad Exchange, one of Google's fastest-growing online display ad products.

If your pause focused on changes to your career or work situation, you may have discovered you are either way off base, slightly out of alignment, or right on track where you are. How well aligned are you with your current company, role, or responsibilities? You may have a sense of this already, but if not, the activities below are designed to help figure this out. Once you have established your alignment, it should be *much* clearer what your next steps are, depending on which scenario relates to you best.

Job Alignment Self-Diagnosis

Think about the job or role you currently hold or most recently held. Write down your thoughts, using the prompts below, in your pausebook.

- What I enjoy most about my company or role:
- What I want to start doing more of:
- What I want to continue doing:
- What I don't want to do or want to minimize in my future role:
- What I envision for myself in my next adventure (recall your strengths, key learnings, and plan of intent):
- How I see myself in my next adventure:

In the Job Alignment Zone

As with any satisfaction survey, what satisfaction rating would you identify with based on your feelings about your current employer and your specific day-to-day job alignment?

Rating 1: Pick one rating for your employer.
Very Unsatisfied | Unsatisfied | Neutral | Satisfied | Very Satisfied

Rating 2: Pick a second one for your specific day-to-day job.
Very Unsatisfied | Unsatisfied | Neutral | Satisfied | Very Satisfied

Assessment

Satisfied or very satisfied with employer *and* role: Congratulations! It's not easy to find employment where you thrive and prosper. Your current company and role hold value for you, and you can continue to build on your success.

No job searches necessary postpause. You managed to take a pause, learn a thing or two, and return all the wiser. Give yourself a big pat on the back. Reenter your job and pick up where you left off. Return refreshed and invigorated with a renewed sense of spirit and purpose.

Satisfied or very satisfied with employer but neutral, unsatisfied, or very unsatisfied with job: While you are satisfied with your employer, something is not working in your day-to-day role. Pausing to discover your yearnings will help you figure out what it is. How can you fulfill those yearnings and be more satisfied? It may mean asking for support from your coworkers, manager, or supporters outside of work, seeking mentorship, and assessing your strengths and what aspects aren't working for you. It may mean learning a new skill to close a skill gap. Take responsibility and ownership to figure it out.

Explore job mobility options inside the company. Every employer is different when it comes to supporting or changing paths within an organization. If there is little to no chance of internal shifts to other roles, have an honest conversation about it with your manager or a trusted confidant. Stay vulnerable. If your career goals will not be met at your existing company, are there other avenues that could help you be more satisfied while staying in your current role? Volunteering in a new field or networking with others informally to learn about a new role or career area may be helpful.

Unsatisfied or very unsatisfied with employer but neutral, satisfied, or very satisfied with job: You may be in a vocation that you love and enjoy your day-to-day work, but you are unsatisfied with how the business is run, its values, or the large organizational inefficiencies you experience.

You're aligned with your role but not your employer. If you think your job aligns with your strengths and purpose, but you are not on board with how your employer operates or its mission or values, I suggest exploring new job opportunities outside your place of employment. Looking elsewhere may result in finding a company that aligns better with your values and strengths. As a conscious and aware employee, you can voice what you think could be improved as you practice TASERing your mental beliefs and chatter while following your yearnings and going for your satisfaction.

I recommend taking action versus staying ambivalent or not doing anything (also a choice). I'm a firm believer that whatever you decide to do, you should feel fulfilled and challenged. Staying present, and noticing your intentions and emotions, is important. It's been said many times, but life *is* short. Change is an important step to getting the most out of life, each and every day. There are many companies out there to feel great about. If you start looking around at new companies, the choice you make to take action may spark ideas about other opportunities. Remember your growth mindset, and stay out of your comfort zone—outside is where the magic, and new opportunities, are found.

Unsatisfied or very unsatisfied with employer *and* neutral, unsatisfied, or very unsatisfied with job: Your strengths, purpose, or actions may not be aligned. Are you exhausting ideas and resources to be satisfied at work?

Something needs to change—is it you? Pausing may help you realize this. Before you explore a new job, ask yourself, "Have I done everything in my current job in order to be satisfied?" This may mean taking responsibility for your actions, having honest conversations with a challenging manager, or doing more in your role to be fulfilled and satisfied. There's not much point in lingering around if you're not satisfied *and* you've exhausted everything you could do to get there. Take a look at how you can serve yourself better—whether it means taking action to be more satisfied in your current role or takings steps to move on and do what makes you satisfied elsewhere.

Pointers for a Successful Job Search

Staying present and intentional during your job search is crucial for finding your next role. Here are a few of my favorite tips that I encourage you to try. You can follow all the suggestions or pick one or two. Each one can result in feeling more secure, confident, and assured that your perfect job will turn up. Commit fully to finding your next job, avoid resting on any laurels, and go all in.

- **Establish your "job search center."** Keep track of your job searches in one place (notebook, document, spreadsheet). It's your go-to resource to track everything job related.

- **Be personable, genuine, and make it easy to say yes.** Put in the extra effort to ensure a successful meeting. Research who you are meeting so you can relate and establish a personal connection. Think of it as putting your own personal touch on any meeting. Imagine you are hosting your interviewer, as if you were hosting him or her in your home or at an event. Every connection counts.

- **Always use one-on-one communication, if you can, versus mass e-mails or form letters.** Do what you can to make it authentic and heartfelt. Express how you feel about your experience or describe the impact this specific individual has had. Customize your message based on what you've learned about them.

- **Create and practice your "elevator pitch" of your current situation (and ideal outcome).** Elevator pitches are usually one or two sentences and convey what you want to achieve through your job search. Write it down and practice saying it consistently. Be bold, and add a specific request, such as, "Do you know anyone you can put me in touch with who might be able to help?" Frame your own experience in terms of transferable skills.

- **Find three words that describe your personal brand.** Add these words to your elevator pitch, résumé headline, or LinkedIn profile.

- **Use an e-calendar for reminders, deadlines, and anything that is time sensitive.** If you plan to apply for a job by Wednesday at 10:00 a.m., create a reminder in your calendar. Slot time to work on what needs to get done before that.

▪ **Keep track of contacts you meet, whether they seem insignificant or vital to your search.** This is great for future reference and for organizing your notes about whom you meet. You can easily identify whom you met with if someone recommends reaching out and can also thank them later when you do find a role. Maybe they played a part. Everyone matters in your job search. Appreciate everyone. They are giving you their time and valuable insights.

▪ **Express gratitude.** Send a gift afterward to everyone who helped you land your job or went above and beyond for you. This can be as easy as a handwritten card, chocolates from your favorite shop, or a gift card for their favorite beverage. Expect nothing in return, and sincerely express your sentiments.

▪ **Create and recite a mantra that motivates you.** Mine was: *From challenge comes opportunity.* Whenever I encountered a challenge, I was reminded it was another opportunity to learn, grow, or realign.

▪ **Stay nourished.** This process can be stressful, overwhelming, and draining. It's important to take care of yourself. Replenish your energy reserves. Practice self-soothing, or do something that nourishes you. It doesn't need to be a lot of time, but it needs to be *quality time.*

▪ **Practice pausing on your job search.** You will have the reserves and energy to move forward every time you renew.

If you can implement a few of these suggestions, your job search has the potential to be a resounding success. It may even be enjoyable. Expect days when you will not want to press on. It is part of your journey. With a little help, organization, intention, and support, you will likely learn a few things while you treat your search as an adventure on the way to finding your ideal next job.

Communicating Effectively Postpause

I am a big believer in the proverb "Words shape the world in which we live." This applies to your communication plan, whether it's to yourself or anyone who supports you. When you stand behind what you believe in, your commitment to yourself and your intention will resonate with others. Every time you have an opportunity to share your truth and do so, you commit to your sense of purpose: pausing is the ideal possible action for yourself, regardless of how long it is, or what you do or don't do. If it helps, think of it like your spiritual marketing plan. Communicate what you believe you are designed to do.

Know Your Audience: Pausers, Helpers, and Sleepers

Everyone you communicate with likely falls into one of three categories: pausers, helpers, and sleepers. Pausers are people who, in some way, have made a shift related to a pause. They are clear and aligned, having gone through a similar experience. They get it. Helpers also get it. Helpers are people who have helped individuals realign through pausing and in some way offered guidance. The third category includes everyone else. Sleepers are "asleep" to their own awareness, emotional facility, and choices. You may have been one before your pause, as I was. They can take action if they are out of alignment, but likely need to be convinced, or they are stuck in their own fear or limiting beliefs that prevent change. Sleepers may be great listeners, but in some aspect they are sleepwalking through life, unaware that they, too, can take action to make a shift.

Pausing has the potential to awaken our own inner sleepers. This is why a communication plan matters. Every interaction is an opportunity to awaken sleepers, align with helpers or become one, or meet like-minded pausers. You never know what you may find or help someone else discover through engaging and sharing your story. Don't be surprised if when you share your pause story someone responds, "I've always wanted to do that." Look these people squarely in the eye and encourage them to test out their own version of it. It doesn't matter if it is a moment or a month of time. You are a catalyst, awakening the sleeper within.

The time has come to communicate your ideas, plans, and takeaways succinctly and successfully with the world. The more you share your truth with others, the more self-validated intimacy you create. The effects of pausing will be even more important to you and others. This goes for whether you communicate to yourself in the mirror or you do it aloud to the casually curious, to work colleagues or your manager, or to those who know you best. Expect and be prepared to explain your motives and situation. They are part of you and who you are becoming.

Remember to be vulnerable, honest, and genuine while being consistent with what feels aligned for you. Whether your pause is a walk around the block or abstaining from your phone for a day or an extended period of time, every interaction in which you can discuss it is an invitation to feel affirmed and let others know how pausing has helped you learn something new. As you share your plan, you will notice others sit up and listen to your eye-opening, authentic update. Your interactions may inspire others to take a pause. Wouldn't that be wonderful?

Tips for Communicating Effectively

1. **Choose an appropriate time and place.** Address your listener in an ideal spot based on your relationship. Choose an environment that helps put you and other people at ease if you sense resistance or scrutiny. It may be your living room, the dinner table, or a park bench.

2. **Express what is meaningful to you, not what others want to hear.** If you're not convinced a pause was the right thing to do, no one else will be, either. Let others know that this was not only what you wanted but what you needed in order to move in the right direction. If you're not met with the support you need, stand strong and recall your purpose and what matters to you. Notice your yearnings and communicate vulnerably so you feel good about what you share.

3. **Let your message sink in with your listener.** Don't worry about silence. If you are not met with support about your decision, reiterate why this was essential for you at this point in time.

4. **Share your purpose.** State what you've been busy doing over the past few days or weeks. This may describe why you decided to take the pause, or what you're planning to change and why. Share your plans and time frame.

5. **Express gratitude.** Thank your listener. Express your

gratitude that this person was open to listening to you and say that you'll be in touch as you continue.

6. **Rehearse out loud until your message is clear.** If you rehearse first, then expressing yourself later to others will feel more natural and less uncomfortable. Notice what you are feeling, and express that, too. Write down what you want to say if it helps organize your thoughts.

PAUSE STORY
Dom Elliott

From Complacent to Growth Mindset Contributor

Dom had been working in the marketing department at YouTube (which is owned by Google) for a few years and felt complacent. He was a prime example of someone being aligned with his employer while also being unsatisfied in his role.

Budget: $3,000 to $5,000

Duration: Three months' unpaid leave of absence

Goal: Travel and determine what the next career move would be

Trigger: Dom didn't feel vested or markedly motivated. He liked his job but no longer felt passionate about his career. Taking some time off seemed like a great way to come up with a plan and weigh his options on what to do next.

Plan: Dom found it relatively easy to share his honest thoughts and feelings with his managers. He had a solid track record at Google, and after he'd made his case, Dom's manager approved of his leave and agreed to keep a spot available on the team once he returned. Dom knew he might look for another role, but only time would tell. He proceeded to make plans to travel to Southeast Asia for about half of his time. The rest would remain unstructured for projects and time to think about what to do next. Dom wanted to look into other interests and possible options for work. He thought about other positions at Google, and other roles in the tech industry. He considered going back to school and getting an MBA. He considered taking classes like programming or computer science, interests he wanted to develop further.

Impact: Dom returned to Google in his previous position, but decided that in the long term he wanted to be closer to technology. His motivating thought was "Everything is incremental." He knew he didn't have to know every step for the next five years. He did know that his first incremental step, his pause, was one step in the right direction.

After a month of searching, Dom landed a role in the developer marketing department for Google Play. He developed a new skill set and pursued a different position with the company. He felt aligned with the new role and what he was focused on: making quality products that serve marketers everywhere. He considered it a fruitful switch, as it leveraged his passion for technology and made him consider future roles in programming, film, or teaching.

He also realized that he could pause again or try new things—he saw nothing as finite or absolute. He took a programming course on his own time once he returned from his break. He also learned screenwriting since he dreamed of writing a movie screenplay. He became a vegetarian. He decided to train for a marathon, a first for him. All of these things were correlated with his pause but not necessarily caused by it.

"I see every decision as one step that leads me to greater happiness," Dom says. "Every little step leads to something new or different I wouldn't have discovered otherwise. I'm taking action because I want to, and no one else is deciding anything for me." Through his time off, Dom learned to reconnect with what makes him feel aligned and fulfilled. As a result, he feels like he lives a life that is rewarding, fulfilling, and engaged on all levels: physical, mental, and emotional.

PRACTICE OF PAUSE ADVICE

Appreciate and notice the incremental steps.
Embrace the journey. It's not about the destination, which may be one big, daunting, finite goal that may initially seem impossible or lofty. Instead, take small steps toward where you want to go. If you're looking for your next career move, spend an hour on the Web looking at job openings or browsing news from companies in your industry.

Avoid getting attached to a specific outcome.
This requires your growth mindset and staying open to the idea that you may have a good excuse to *not* do something. Challenge your assumptions. Have a conversation with a stranger. Stay curious. If you're not familiar with someone or something, that is a reason to look deeper at it, not to avoid it.

Gain perspective outside of your day-to-day routine.
This allows the opportunity to think differently and develop new perspectives and ideas as your mind adapts to a new environment.

Practice of Pause Moments:
Chapter 11

What are your biggest takeaways from your time off?
Write or sticky note them on your refrigerator, front door, or bathroom mirror. Spend time each day integrating your takeaways by reading them and asking yourself how you are acting, feeling, and behaving differently postpause.

How did you grow or what is different as a result of your pause takeaways?
Celebrate what you learned and how you grew. Plan some self-soothing, and go for feeling fulfilled and satisfied in something you enjoy.

How will you/did you transition from your pause?
How do you want to feel and be during this time, and how much time is needed? Any other requirements for your transition?

Create your own job search center.
You can access an example spreadsheet and make a copy at www.rachaelomeara.com.

Draft your communication plan.
What feels vulnerable or risky for you to say? What resonates with what you learned or how you plan to shift? Incorporate all of these into your communication plan.

Chapter 12

Pausing as a Way of Life

*The minute you begin to do what you really want to do,
it's really a different kind of life.*

— R. BUCKMINSTER FULLER

PAUSING IS A global conversation and movement that is becoming louder, more important, and necessary as our world marches on at an accelerated pace. Without the awareness gained from pausing how do you know how you feel, what matters, or what aligns? For the past five years, I have embraced the power of pausing and the lessons it's taught me. I have felt compelled, *obligated*, to share what I learned to help anyone who feels stuck, lost, or mentally inadequate due to circumstances at work or in their personal life that don't seem to make sense anymore. I want to make pausing an acceptable and empowering way of life. I see it as a commonly used word in our modern lexicon. "How are you pausing today? What did you learn on your last pause? How was it meaningful?"

You know pausing can span a few short breaths or a lifetime. It requires awareness, courage, and stillness. It is the solace that guides you to return to your center and align with your soul if you've gotten off track. If you are on track, it helps you stay that way. It is that intentional shift in behavior to do something different. It means being ready for what comes next and knowing you are okay in the unknown. It is the wisdom of knowing that pausing fuels your forward momentum.

Potential Transformation

I first learned about the two main types of energy in high school physics. I won't get too geeky, but bear with me. Kinetic energy is defined as energy in use, while potential energy is defined as the stored energy of an object. Conceptually, pausing is potential energy. Every time you pause, your potential energy can be restored. It could be a moment to notice your emotions, six short breaths, or any restorative behavior. The conservation of energy principle tells us that energy can be changed from one form to another and that it cannot be created or destroyed. If we apply this concept to pausing, whatever action follows your pause *transforms* your potential energy into kinetic energy. And it's not just your energy that can transform—*you* can transform. The way you think, behave, and feel can all be shifted based on what you discover while pausing.

The Six Skills of Transformation

Pausing started me on a transformational journey that continues to evolve. Earlier I quoted transformational educator Jack Mezirow saying that adulthood is meant for transformation. Pausing can be a gateway or a catalyst that leads to your transformation. When I think about my ongoing journey, I see how pausing took me through the six skills of transformation, described below, developed by Drs. Judith and Bob Wright.[1] Each of us can apply this model to our own lives and use tools and resources that work best to get us there. Pausing can also become a way of life and a tool toward staying aligned on our personal path.

The six steps are a road map to reference where you are at any given time. This isn't a linear process; you may cycle through these steps over and over again before, during, and after your pause. They're useful not only while pausing, but applied to any situation. The key is to continue to yearn and engage to fulfill your deepest desires that serve you. As I look at my own pause journey and continue to pause, I recognize my feelings, notice my thoughts, and shift my behavior, all referencing these six steps. You can do the same.

1. **Yearn.** What do you yearn for? Pausing allows the space and the time to figure out how to meet your yearnings and recognize and address limiting beliefs and mental chatter. Pausing is a chance to create the space to discover what your yearnings are, and the time to be with yourself.

2. **Engage.** Respond to urges generated by your deeper yearnings. Be spontaneous. Take action to fulfill or satisfy a deeper hunger. Notice how you feel and express yourself. Ask others how they see you. Engage and meet your yearnings. I engaged by asking for time off from work. I asked others how I could contribute. Take action to intentionally figure out next steps.

3. **Reveal.** How you think about things differently is the revealing stage sometimes referred to as "revelating."

What are you aware of or what are you learning from your experience? What can you be curious about or how can you bring your growth mindset to pausing? You do not need to live in a container you created previously: your lifestyle, your way of being, your rules and beliefs. You can change all of them, and as you build in new lessons and insights from time spent meeting your yearnings, you enhance your power to do so.

4. **Liberate.** When you think (reveal) differently, you do things differently and liberate yourself. Get out of your comfort zone and try new things. What new action or behavior is possible based on how you yearn, engage, and reveal new ways of thinking about things? Take some risks. In doing so, you create new habits and routines. New pathways pop up that you can go down, such as expressing something new or facing a fear and taking action. Follow new bread crumbs, which may lead to new discoveries or skills.

5. **Rematrix.** Rematrixing is the act of creating new neural pathways by thinking and doing things differently. As you shift your thoughts, behavior, and actions as a result of pausing, your neural networks can change. This process, and its repetition, creates your new neural pathways and, over time, can lead to long-term sustainable transformational change.

6. **Dedicate.** Commit to pausing as a way of life. By continually tuning in to your inner voice, you establish a regular practice to learn more about yourself. In my case, I took on new challenges to write about pausing and combine it with my work in emotional intelligence so I can help others lead more satisfying

lives. I am committed to helping others grow from the power of pause so that they, too, are more connected with themselves, discover their yearnings, and transform.

Pausing can be integrated into your everyday life. It's the opposite of rushing into anything. After all, pausing is about being. Right now, pause for a moment and ask yourself, "What would I do if I had one moment, one hour, one day, or even one week, to pause?"

What would you say?
How would you feel?
Who would you be with?
What would be different?

That is the power of pause.

Twentieth-century existentialist author and poet Rainer Maria Rilke had a wonderful take on the unknown, which he embraced and adopted as his own mantra: "Embrace that, live that and hopefully you will live yourself into the answers." In his book *Letters to a Young Poet*, he reminds us that we don't need to have everything figured out. Rather, why not live a full life and let the answers unfold.

I would like to beg you, dear Sir, as well as I can, to have patience with everything unresolved in your heart and to try to love the questions themselves as if they were locked rooms or books written in a very foreign language. Don't search for the answers, which could not be given to you now, because you would not be able to live them. And the point is, to live everything. Live the questions now. Perhaps then, someday far in the future, you will gradually, without even noticing it, live your way into the answer.[2]

Like Rilke reminds us, live yourself into the answers. You don't need to have all the answers, even though most of us quiver at the idea of not having everything figured out. The practice of pausing is one way to let the answers unfold naturally. As you shift, you allow them to emerge.

Practice of Pause Moments:
Chapter 12

How can you integrate pausing into your lifestyle? What does it look like? How can you pause throughout your day to shift your perspective or behavior?

How do you see yourself moving through the six skills of transformation? What do you yearn for and how do you engage to fulfill and satisfy those yearnings? How are you thinking (reveal) and acting (liberate) differently as a result? What has shifted for you, and how are you choosing to continue to make shifts (dedicate)?

Notes

INTRODUCTION

1. "2011 employee benefits report." Society for Human Resource Management (SHRM) Online. 2011. www.shrm.org/Research/SurveyFindings/Articles/Documents/2011_Emp_Benefits_Report.pdf (accessed July 7, 2006).

CHAPTER 2

1. Wright, Bob. "AC72 Leadership Master's Capstone Discussion." Lecture. Wright Graduate University, Elkhorn, WI. July 10, 2016.
2. Wright, Judith, and Bob Wright. 2016. *The Heart of the Fight: A Couple's Guide to Fifteen Common Fights, What They Really Mean, and How They Can Bring You Closer.* Oakland, CA: New Harbinger, 64.
3. Ibid., 72–73.
4. Ibid., 72.
5. Wright, Judith, and Bob Wright. 2013. *Transformed! The Science of Spectacular Living.* Nashville, TN: Turner, 193.

6. Ibid., 31.
7. Wright and Wright, *The Heart of the Fight*, 77.
8. Ibid., 65.
9. Wright, Judith. 2006. *The Soft Addiction Solution: Break Free of the Seemingly Harmless Habits That Keep You from the Life You Want*. New York: Jeremy P. Tarcher/Penguin.
10. Beames, Thomas B. 1992. *A Student's Glossary of Adlerian Terminology*. Ladysmith, BC: Photon.

CHAPTER 3

1. Campbell, Joseph. 1972. *The Hero With a Thousand Faces*. Princeton, NJ: Princeton University Press.
2. Tillich, Paul. 1952. *The Courage to Be*. New Haven, CT: Yale University Press.
3. *Merriam-Webster Online Dictionary*, s.v. "courage." www.merriam-webster.com/dictionary/courage.
4. Durst, Gary Michael. 1982. *Management by Responsibility*. Evanston, IL: G. M. Durst.
5. Frankl, Viktor E. 2006. *Man's Search for Meaning*. Boston: Beacon Press.
6. Brown, Brené. 2015. *Rising Strong*. New York: Spiegel and Grau, 85–88, 218.
7. Dweck, Carol S. 2006. *Mindset: The New Psychology of Success*. New York: Random House.
8. Klauser, Henriette Anne. 2000. *Write It Down, Make It Happen: Knowing What You Want—And Getting It!* New York: Scribner.
9. "VSL: SCIENCE: The two-minute plan for feeling better." *Observer*, March 2, 2009. http://observer.com/2009/03/effects-brief-writing-health/ (accessed July 12, 2016).
10. Niemiec, Ryan M. "5 key tips for finding happiness at work." *Psychology Today*, March 6, 2015. www.psychologytoday.com/blog/what-matters-most/201503/5-key-tips-finding-happiness-work (accessed July 8, 2016).
11. McQuaid, Michelle. "Strengths challenge." http://strengthschallenge.com/ (accessed July 4, 2016).
12. Sethi, Ramit, and Jeff Kuo. "Earn $1000 on the side." Module 1 lesson 2. Pick your field. Earn1k.com. http://earn1k.com (accessed July 4, 2016).

13. Schnarch, David Morris. 2012. *Passionate Marriage: Keeping Love and Intimacy Alive in Committed Relationships*. Brunswick, Victoria, Australia: Scribe.
14. *Online Etymology Dictionary*, s.v. "busy." www.etymonline.com/index.php?allowed_in_frame=0&search=busy (accessed July 4, 2016).
15. *Merriam-Webster Online Dictionary*, s.v. "busy." www.merriam-webster.com/dictionary/busy (accessed July 4, 2016).
16. Jabr, Ferris. "Why your brain needs more downtime." *Scientific American*. Oct. 15, 2013. www.scientificamerican.com/article/mental-downtime/.
17. "Coherence." HeartMath Institute. Nov. 11, 2012. www.heartmath.org/articles-of-the-heart/the-math-of-heartmath/coherence/#more-5762.

CHAPTER 4

1. Mezirow, Jack. 2000. *Learning as Transformation: Critical Perspectives on a Theory in Progress*. San Francisco: Jossey-Bass.
2. Wright and Wright, *The Heart of the Fight*, 105, 108.
3. Bowlby, John. 1988. *A Secure Bbase: Clinical Applications of Attachment Theory*. London: Routledge.
4. Wright and Wright, *Transformed!*, 4.
5. Cozolino, Louis J. 2006. *The Neuroscience of Human Relationships: Attachment and the Developing Social Brain*. New York: Norton, 307.
6. Wright and Wright, *Transformed!*, 130–31.
7. Siegel, Daniel J. 2010. *Mindsight: The New Science of Personal Transformation*. New York: Bantam, 14–15.
8. Ericsson, K. A., R. T. Krampe, and C. Tesch-Römer. 1993. "The role of deliberate practice in the acquisition of expert performance." *Psychological Review* 100, vol. 3, 393–94.
9. Brach, Tara. 2003. *Radical Acceptance: Embracing Your Life with the Heart of a Buddha*. New York: Bantam.
10. "William James." Pursuit of Happiness. www.pursuit-of-happiness.org/history-of-happiness/william-james/ (accessed Sept. 24, 2016).
11. James, William, and Giles B. Gunn. 2000. *Pragmatism and Other Writings*. New York: Penguin Books, 240.

CHAPTER 5

1. Pomerleau, Kyle. "2016 tax brackets." Tax Foundation. http://taxfoundation.org/article/2016-tax-brackets (accessed July 4, 2016).

CHAPTER 6

1. Wright, Bob. "AC72 leadership and AC42 purposeful living group discussion." Lecture. Wright Graduate University, Elkhorn, WI. July 9, 2016.
2. Ibid.
3. Frankl, *Man's Search for Meaning.*
4. Bernstein, Gabrielle. "You don't have time to meditate?" Gabbybernstein.com. http://gabbyb.tv/vlogging/you-dont-have-time-to-meditate (accessed July 4, 2016).
5. Keller, David King. "MicroMindfulness: Towards an accessible mindfulness-based stress reduction practice." PhD diss., California Institute of Integral Studies, 2014.

CHAPTER 7

1. Meeker, Mary, and Liang Wu. "2013 Internet trends." KPCB.com. www.kpcb.com/blog/2013-internet-trends (accessed July 4, 2016).
2. Enoch, Glenn. "The Nielsen total audience report Q1 2016." Nielsen.com. www.nielsen.com/content/dam/corporate/us/en/reports-downloads/2016-reports/total-audience-report-q1-2016.pdf (accessed July 4, 2016).
3. "The U.S. digital consumer report." Nielsen.com. Feb. 2, 2014. www.nielsen.com/us/en/insights/reports/2014/the-us-digital-consumer-report.html (accessed July 4, 2016).
4. Ibid.
5. Ibid.
6. Wright, *The Soft Addiction Solution*, 64.
7. *Oxford Dictionaries*, s.v. "digital detox." www.oxforddictionaries.com/us/definition/american_english/digital-detox (accessed July 4, 2016).
8. Shlain, Tiffany. 2012. *Brain power: From Neurons to Networks.* n.p.: TED Conferences.

9. Huffington, Arianna. 2014. *Thrive: The Third Metric to Redefining Success and Creating a Life of Well-being, Wisdom, and Wonder.* New York: Harmony, 6.
10. Ibid., 81.
11. Hill, Simon. "Is blue light keeping you up at night?" *Digital Trends.* July 26, 2015. www.digitaltrends.com/mobile/does -blue-light-ruin-sleep-we-ask-an-expert/#ixzz3uEtzwHFZ (accessed July 4, 2016).

CHAPTER 8

1. "Paid time off programs and practices." WorldAtWork.org. June 2016, www.worldatwork.org/waw/adimLink?id=80292 (accessed July 5, 2016).
2. Shen, Lucinda. "These 19 great employers offer paid sabbaticals." Fortune.com. http://fortune.com/2016/03/07/best -companies-to-work-for-sabbaticals/ (accessed July 6, 2016).
3. *Wikipedia*, s.v. "limbic system." https://en.wikipedia.org/wiki/ Limbic_system (accessed July 6, 2016).
4. O'Meara, Rachael. "Unpaid leave survey." Google Consumer Surveys. Dec. 8, 2015.
5. Kallayil, Gopi. 2015. *The Internet to the Inner-net: Five Ways to Reset Your Connection and Live a Conscious Life.* Carlsbad, CA: Hay House.
6. Blackstone, Judith. 2012. *Belonging Here: A Guide for the Spiritually Sensitive Person.* Boulder, CO: Sounds True.
7. Ram Dass. 1971. *Be Here Now, Remember.* San Cristobal, NM: Lama Foundation.

CHAPTER 9

1. Jobs, Steve. "Stanford 2005 commencement speech." www. youtube.com/watch?v=zfZfVXIJRXI (accessed July 6, 2016).
2. Allen, David. 2001. *Getting Things Done: The Art of Stress-free Productivity.* New York: Viking, 10.
3. Lambert, Craig. 1998. *Mind Over Water: Lessons on Life from the Art of Rowing.* Boston: Houghton Mifflin.

CHAPTER 10

1. Wright, Judith. "Nourishment and self-care techniques." Discussion. Year of Transformation Nourishment and Self-Care Weekend, Wright Foundation, Chicago. July 30–31, 2016.
2. Gollwitzer, Peter M., and Paschal Sheeran. 2009. "Self-regulation of consumer decision making and behavior: The role of implementation intentions." *Journal of Consumer Psychology* 19 (2009): 593–607. Konstanz: Bibliothek der Universität Konstanz.
3. Wright and Wright, *The Heart of the Fight*, 160.
4. Rankin, Lissa. "About me in 30 seconds." Lissarankin.com http://lissarankin.com/about/ (accessed Sept. 24, 2016).
5. Eisenstein, Charles. "2013: The space between stories." Charleseisenstein.net. http://charleseisenstein.net/2013-the -space-between-stories/ (accessed July 6, 2016).
6. Wright, Bob. "Living with purpose." Wright Foundation. Year of Transformation Week 8 Handout. June 19, 2013.
7. Rath, Tom. 2007. *StrengthsFinder 2.0*. New York: Gallup Press.
8. Bernstein, Gabrielle. 2011. *Spirit Junkie: A Radical Road to Discovering Self-love and Miracles*. New York: Harmony Books.
9. Ibid.

CHAPTER 12

1. Wright and Wright, *Transformed!*, 31–33.
2. Rilke, Rainer Maria, Franz Xaver Kappus, and Joan M. Burnham. 2000. *Letters to a Young Poet*. Novato, CA: New World Library.

Further Resources

Many of the concepts in this book are taken from my studies of transformational leadership and coaching at the Wright Graduate University for the Realization of Human Potential. Below are some recommended resources and ideas for additional reading. More online resources and end-of-chapter exercises are available on my Web site, www.rachaelomeara.com, including video and audio links where applicable.

CHAPTER 2

Wright Foundation Web sites: www.judithwright.com, www.wright living.com, www.wrightgrad.edu, www.thewrightfoundation.org

Training weekend to unleash your potential: Whether you're looking to advance in your career by being a stronger leader, assert yourself more aggressively, date more successfully, or build stronger relationships with your children, this powerful weekend seminar lays the foundation for lifelong learning and fulfillment of your greatest potential. Register for an upcoming training using the code REMATRIX at http://foundationsweekendtraining.com/.

Alfred Adler (1870–1937) is recognized as the founder of individual psychology and an entire branch of psychology known as Adlerian theory. He wrote dozens of books, including *Understanding Human Nature*. He came up with the three major areas of life, lifestyle analysis, life project, apperception, and much more. Entire lexicons have been created based on his work. Many schools teach his work, including the Adler Graduate School: http://alfred adler.edu/about/theory.

CHAPTER 4

Mike Robbins Web site: http://mike-robbins.com/

CHAPTER 5

Don't Break the Bank worksheet "Pause Resources" Web page at: www.rachaelomeara.com/pauseresources

Jenny Blake books, workshops, and coaching: http://www.jenny blake.me/

Alfie van der Zwan Mindful365 mobile app provides daily contemplations, one for each day of the year: http://mindful365.com/

CHAPTER 6

Gabby Bernstein Web site: http://gabbybernstein.com/

Austin Hill Shaw Web site: www.austinhillshaw.com

Mark Thornton *Meditation in a New York Minute* contains a series of eighteen practical awareness exercises that anyone can do, multiple times a day. It's how I was introduced to meditation. It's an easy read and available as an audiobook. (Disclaimer: I am on Mark's board for his nonprofit, Business for the Planet.)

CHAPTER 7

Common Sense Media is a great free resource for adults/parents to navigate children's consumption of media, while helping kids thrive in a world of media and technology. The group empowers parents, teachers, and policymakers by providing unbiased information, trusted advice, and tools to help them harness the power of media and technology as a positive force in all kids' lives. Kids can use it, too. Visit www.commonsensemedia.org/ or mobile app ratings/reviews for kids media apps.

Tiffany Shlain: Tech Shabbat infographic: www.moxieinstitute.org/technology_shabbats

Moxie Institute Web site: www.moxieinstitute.org

Friday App from rebooters.net (available in Apple iTunes) and www.thefridayapp.com/

Danielle LaPorte books, products, Web site: www.daniellelaporte.com

Arianna Huffington has assembled a thorough and helpful list of resources for curbing distractions in the appendix of her book *Thrive*.

CHAPTER 9

Joe Kutchera Web site, consulting, book info: http://joekutchera.com/

Joe's recommended reading:

Transitions: Making Sense of Life's Changes by William Bridges provides readers with a summary of the emotional process and evolution that we go through during major life changes like losing a job, moving, or changing careers. I found this book enormously helpful in understanding the process of going through my own transition.

The 4-Hour Workweek by Timothy Ferris boldly encourages today's knowledge workers to negotiate a "semi-sabbatical" with current employers or to work virtually so they can take on big passion projects like writing a book, surfing, or learning a new language while balancing work responsibilities.

Flawless Consulting: A Guide to Getting Your Expertise Used by Peter Block inspires us to set up a solo consultancy, focus our business on our core specialties, get clients, and enjoy the freedom of being a "solopreneur."

CHAPTER 10

Dr. Lissa Rankin has led two National Public Television (PBS) specials and leads classes at retreat centers like Esalen and Kripalu. To read more about her journey, visit LissaRankin.com and her page on Facebook where she blogs regularly. For info on the Whole

Health Medicine Institute visit http://wholehealthmedicine
institute.com/.

Steve Sisgold coaching, consulting, books; Web site: www.whole
bodyintelligence.com

StrengthsFinder 2.0: For test and access code of the comprehensive
overview, visit www.strengthstest.com/strengths-tests/strengths
finder-20-access-code.html. You have an option on this site to
complete a detailed version for your relative dominance in each
strength (cost: $89.99).

CHAPTER 11

Job search center concept is from Jen Petroff, a Google colleague.
Jen introduced me to her "job command search center" and "job
fire drill article" during my job search. It is what I based my job
search template on, combined with what she mentioned in her
article.

For a detailed job search center template inspired by Jen's article visit
my Web site: www.rachaelomeara.com/pauseresources.

Gratitude

I would like to express my deepest thanks to the following individuals:

Holly Payne, your edits and insights gave birth to a book beyond what I could have imagined.

My editing and publishing allies: Erin Malone and WME, you are an awesome agent and a blessing who always believed in *Pause* from day one. My editors Jeanette Shaw and Lauren Appleton and the stellar TarcherPerigee team, you are top notch for editorial excellence. You made editing with your critical eye and high standards look easy. Barbara and the CaveHendricks team. Lea Saslav, thank you for your strategy and PR know-how. Arianna Huffington, thank you for your intros and inviting me to share my story and believing in the power of *Pause*. Pause and Thrive!

Sarab Khurana, thanks for your love and shining light.

Your support through the editing process and school was kind of a big deal. I love you much.

My family members far and wide: Drew, I am blessed to have you as my brother, fellow transformer. Mom and Dick and the Isbell clan, thanks for all your support and love. Dad, I am enjoying our new relationship. Luke, I will always have a biscuit for you. To my Canadian counterparts, the Mays and Lowes, thanks for your support.

The Wright Foundation community: Thank you for facilitating my emergence and inspiring me moment by moment. Dr. Bob and Dr. Judith, you are helping me become someone I couldn't have imagined. I stand on your shoulders along with the scholar practitioners you introduced me to. Thank you lab members and leaders of Higher Ground, Tuesday Tigers, Pythons, and Wright Graduate University faculty, fellow students, and mentors, especially Molly Vaile, Grace Kavadoy, Monica Stacco, and my coach Beryl Stromsa.

My NYAC rowing friends and family and those who share my passion: You know who you are.

Googlers past and present: Maya Watts and our Advertising Solutions Team. Woot! If it wasn't for your high bar for excellence, *Pause* would not exist. Jeremy Woodlee and Chip Hall and our entire team, thank you! Jane Hong, thanks for casually mentioning that your old role was available. Gopi Kallayil, Punit Aggarwal, Paul Santagata, Becky Cotton, and Sue McCauley, your passion, talents, and dedication inspire me.

Talks@ authors, SIY crew, gPausers, Women@leads: You make work life better and more fun for everyone.

Mark Thornton, you helped me find a lot of what I needed. Whether it was a practice, a person, or a meal at the Otic Oasis cantina, I am tremendously grateful for everything you've brought my way.

Mystic Sisters Lissa Rankin, Sarah Drew, Tosha Silver, Crystallin Dillon, Ariane de Bonvoisin, Ania Fizyta, Amina Zimani, Edda Coscioni, Megan Taylor, Christine Arylo, Karen Jones, Gwen Elliot, Syl Rochet, Deepika Bajaj, Samantha Sutton, Cathy Goerz, and Emily Jennings.

Alex Conn, Matt Klein, Shir Nir, thank you for your support and being pause-some allies.

Those willing to share their story in this book and who contributed to *Pause*: Thank you for inspiring others through your courage to shift your behavior and helping me shift mine.

To those I knew before, during, and after my pause who supported and continue to support me.

Those who know that transforming the world starts with you and who are curious to know more.

Spirit, you always have my back and I am eternally grateful. Thank you. Thank you. Thank you.

Index

About the Author

Rachael O'Meara is a transformational leadership and executive coach, assisting others to fulfill their potential. She works at Google and also hosts authors who have meaningful messages about mindfulness and emotional intelligence for the Talks at Google YouTube channel. She writes regularly for various outlets, including the *Huffington Post*, and leads workshops and speaks on the practice of pausing. She is also a Search Inside Yourself Facilitator (SIYLI.org). She is certified in Transformational Coaching from the Wright Graduate University for the Realization of Human Potential (ICF certified), and has an MBA from Fordham University. Rachael currently lives in San Francisco, where she is working on being and pausing.

www.rachaelomeara.com

facebook.com/rachaelmomeara

@romeara1